JAINA RELATIVISM AND RELATIVITY PHYSICS

India's Scientific Heritage

Founder Editor : Late Dr L M Singhvi

General Editor
DR. S N BHAVSAR

Guest Editor
ROBERT W. BOYER

16

JAINA RELATIVISM AND RELATIVITY PHYSICS

JAYANT BURDE

MOTILAL BANARSIDASS PUBLISHERS
PRIVATE LIMITED • DELHI

First Edition: Delhi : 2014

ISBN : 978-81-208-3815-4

MOTILAL BANARSIDASS
41 U.A. Bungalow Road, Jawahar Nagar, Delhi 110007
8 Mahalaxmi Chamber, 22 Bhulabhai Desai Road, Mumbai 400026
203 Royapettah High Road, Mylapore, Chennai 600004
236, 9th Main III Block, Jayanagar, Bengaluru 560011
Sanas Plaza, 1302 Baji Rao Road, Pune 411002
8 Camac Street, Kolkata 700017
Ashok Rajpath, Patna 800004
Chowk, Varanasi 221001

Printed in India
by RP Jain at NAB Printing Unit,
A-44, Naraina Industrial Area, Phase-I, New Delhi-110028
and published by JP Jain for Motilal Banarsidass Publishers (P) Ltd,
41 U.A. Bungalow Road, Jawahar Nagar, Delhi-110007

For

Pushpa (Meena) and Jayant

Foreword

Jaina Relativism and Relativity Physics by Jayant Burde, Nashik is a solid contribution to modern scholarship in the important work of linking ancient and modern sciences, and I am honored by the invitation to introduce it. Its key task seems to be an examination of the relationship of relativism and non-absolutism in Jainism with Einstein's Theories of Relativity, a useful one to carry out.

I do not have the background to comment on the book's contents on the ancient and valued tradition of Jainism. But it does seem from my limited study of relativity theories to present these theories in a clarifying style, especially for readers not trained in the language of mathematical physics. I thought that in this Foreword it also might be useful to introduce a rationale for how ancient subjective knowledge systems could have addressed key current issues long before the rich experimental methodologies and findings in contemporary science were developed and applied.

Objective and subjective approaches to gain knowledge

Logical reasoning and ordinary sensory experience from the outer, indirect, third-person perspective as an *objective experimental* approach has been the primary means to gain knowledge in modern science.This can be contrasted with the direct, first-person means as a *subjective experiential* approach in ancient traditions. These means to gain knowledge historically separated western and eastern sciences. The long-standing western classical objective approach of not including mind and consciousness—which are central in the ancient subjective approach—is now becoming recognized as fundamentally fragmented and as having been inadequate all along. Western classical science tacitly assumed subjective logical consistency within and across observers as core to the scientific method, without acknowledging this foundational consistency and its implications for the reality of mind and consciousness. This has led to a view of human nature as absent inherent meaning or free will.

Modern science has finally progressed to the stage where it is recognizing the necessity of including mind and consciousness for a coherent explanation of even physical reality. There are now inklings of an integration of the two approaches into a more unified understanding and experience of nature. This is a profound and most fortunate development. The additional means to gain knowledge emphasized in ancient traditions—such as in the ancient Vedic tradition of *Yoga* with which I am most familiar—had been overlooked in modern science.

To protect against unreliable subjectivity in reason and ordinary sensory experience, the objectivescientific method has relied upon consensual validation, or public agreement. But it is important to recognize that consensus is based on the level of functioning of those who contribute to it.The entire enterprise of *objective* science is based primarily on reason and experience in the ordinary waking state of consciousness. This state is the phenomenological basis for the independence of observed (object) and observer (subject) that is tacitly imposed on nature in the ordinary waking state. Modern science is based on object-subject duality because experiences of modern scientists have been for the most part restricted to the ordinary waking state. And there has been almost no recognition of this state-dependent limitation.

The assumption that physical objects are the only objects existing in nature has been a basic tenet of physical theory in objective science. It is drawn from the belief based on ordinary sensory experience that objects we can hear, touch, see, taste, and smell are the only ontologically real objects, existing objectively independent of our subjective minds. In this view, the mind-body problem and the link between subjective and objective were presumed to be resolved, because the mind eventually will be completely accounted for by physical brain processes. This reduced scientific research to the search for the essence of matter, which eventually would account for mind—if correct.

In this physical worldview, nature is structured in layers from macroscopic to microscopic atomic, nuclear, and sub-nuclear layers. Objective investigation has involved reductive probing of smaller time and distance scales and higher energy and temperature states, in search of the essence of matter. The range of scales can be characterized as follows:

Ultramacroscopic levels: Infinity to cosmic expanse
Macroscopic levels: cosmic expanse to $\sim 10^{-3}$ cm
Microscopic levels: $\sim 10^{-3}$ cm to $\sim 10^{-8}$ cm
Ultramicroscopic levels: $\sim 10^{-8}$ cm to $\sim 10^{-33}$ cm
Unified field level: $\sim 10^{-33}$ cm or infinitesimal to Infinity

The resolving power of our ordinary senses for direct sensory observation is in the comparatively limited macroscopic range. The wavelength of visible light for example is in the range of 10^{-4} cm, too wide to observe directly anything smaller than a cell. Visual observation has been extended with the aid of probing tools such as the electron microscope to about 10^{-8} cm, still larger than an atomic nucleus. In other words, no one yet has directly seen an atom in detail, but indirect evidence for it is considered extensive.

In the past century, modern science has progressed to time and distance scales far smaller than can be experienced directly through the ordinary senses. Reductive investigations analyzed matter to atomic, sub-atomic, nuclear, and sub-nuclear particles. All motion involved matter particles bumping into each other—the 'billiard ball' model of causality. Eventually it was recognized that this model couldn't explain phenomena such as what holds sub-atomic particles into atoms, and how some atoms fall apart by radiating sub-atomic particles. As indirect investigations in physics as well as neuroscience have gone from macroscopic tangible localized matter to theorized underlying abstract quantum fields, the *interdependence* of object and observer increasingly has encroached upon classical scientific objectivity and the object-subject gap. Research in quantum field theory is now challenging the long-held view of the independence of object (matter, body) and subject (mind) that has been a core principle in objective science. Matter and mind, object and subject, physics and psychology, can no longer be considered independent, in light of recent advances.

Progress toward a real level of mind in nature

Modern scientific theories are now developing that recognize the necessity of additional non-physical levels of nature where real minds might actually exist. The view of only physical layers of nature as real is inadequate, and an additional 'metric' of levels of interdependence and entanglement as more fundamental to the structure of nature is emerging. Concepts of *information space* and *quantum mind* as real levels of nature underlying the physical level of nature reflect this progress on the forefront of quantum field theories. A key issue in this progress is how nonlocal, nonphysicalprocesses link to the local physical brain—which can be understood to be a new version of the old mind-body problem.

Ancient knowledge traditions have long recognized the *interdependence* of objectivity and subjectivity, matter and mind, physical and mental. This is necessary for a logical account of free will, and for understanding how to gain valid knowledge directly through reliable subjective means—in the inner laboratory of the conscious mind of the scientist. Systematic first-person means to gain knowledge in the *Yoga* aspect of the Vedic tradition, for example, facilitates higher development beyond the ordinary waking state to experiences of subtler underlying levels of nature that can link mind and matter. This is the missing holistic ingredient in modern scientific epistemology. Recognition and direct experience of these subtler levels and the transcendent level is crucial to advance the more integrated view of nature being hinted at in cutting edge quantum theories that are progressing toward unified field theory.

This book seems to bring out well the compatibility of modern relativity theories and Jain relativistic perspectives. A specific point of clarification, however, is that although at one phase of Einstein's investigations into the relativity of spacetime he did argue strongly against the concept of a 'luminiferous aether,' as noted in this book, he apparently came back to it but just not as an absolute standard for motion (Brian Greene, *The fabric of the cosmos,* 2004. p. 76). In his May 5, 1920 talk at the University of Leyden, Germany, Einstein commented: "More careful reflection teaches us... that the Special Theory of Relativity does not compel us to deny the Aether. We may assume the existence of an Aether; only we must give up ascribing a definite state of motion to it..."

As a final point on further work in the useful direction this book is taking, it would be a huge contribution if the author delved further into the correspondence of ancient and modern sciences by addressing contemporary dilemmas in quantum and unified field theories. Of particular benefit would be to examine topics beyond relativity theory to cutting edge theories of information space, quantum mind, unified field theory, and their relationship to consciousness. Such topics are dealt with in different ways in ancient traditions, such as for example in the six Vedic Darshanas (Nyaya, Vaishesika, Sankhya, Yoga, Purva Mimansa, Vedanta) only briefly commented upon in this book. A deeper consideration of how the holistic Vedic account unifies relative and absolute would be helpful for a more complete view.

It is my pleasure to thank Jayant Burde for his contribution to modern scholarship reflected in this useful book.

RW Boyer, PhD

Contents

Preface

Einstein's theory of relativity appeared in the early twentieth century. The theory of special relativity was published in 1905 and that of general relativity appeared in 1915. The theory shook many fundamental concepts of physics such as space, time, mass and energy. The shock waves of the theory were not confined to physics, they were felt in almost all the branches of science, philosophy and even literature.

Unfortunately, the theory spawned many misconceptions. Lay persons asserted, "Everything is relative", "You can go back in time". Those who were familiar with the western as well as eastern philosophy of relativism or relativity or non-absolutism claimed, "Our ancestors talked about relativity long back" or "Our forebears had anticipated Einstein long ago". Most of these misperceptions stem form the fact that Einstein uses the word "relativity" for his theory in physics.

Undoubtedly there are many theories of philosophical relativity. They assert non-absolutism of knowledge. Most of these theories are idealist which deny objective cognition and contend that human knowledge does not reflect the objective world.

In Jaina relativism called *anekāntavāda* or *syādvāda* one finds a rare combination of non-absolutism and objectivity. *Anekāntavāda* is one of the main pillars of Jaina philosophy and religion. It believes in rationality, objectivity and like science relies on empirical evidence.

This book is a comparative study of philosophical relativism with special reference to Jaina non-absolutism on the one hand and relativity physics on the other. It identifies similarities as well as differences between these two apparently disparate branches of knowledge.

I hope the analysis will dispel many misconceptions about relativity physics. It should also help the reader understand the extent of parallelism between Jaina non-absolutism and Einstein's theory.

I have tried to keep the level of mathematics in relativity physics as low as possible and only the well-known formulas, which are absolutely necessary are included. These are explained in ordinary language and the reader need not memorize them.

Pronunciation of Sanskrit/Indic Phonemes and Words

1. Sanskrit vowels are pure such as are found in French, Italian and Spanish. (a, i, u, ṛ, ḷ) are short while (ā, ī, ū, ṝ, ḹ, e, o, ai, au) are long.
2. A dental consonant is one in which the tip of the tongue presses against the upper teeth.
3. A retroflex sound is pronounced with the tongue-tip curled back.
4. An aspirate is a consonant followed by the sound of 'h' e.g. gh in doghouse.
5. It is necessary to know the sounds only to recognize their basic differences. It is not necessary to pronounce the words exactly as Indians do, unless one is learning Sanskrit or an Indic language.
6. Some Indic languages have also borrowed certain sounds from Dravidian languages. These are omitted to avoid complications.

a f*u*n

ā *a*rm

ai *ai*sle (approximate)

au c*ow* (approximate)

b *b*ear

bh aspirated b as in a*bh*or

c *ch*est

ch aspirated as in chur*chh*ill
ḍ *d*en, but retroflex
d *d*en but dental similar to th in *th*en
ḍh aspirated ḍ resembling dh in a*dh*ere
dh aspirated d
e pl*ay*
g give
gh aspirated g, as in do*gh*ouse
ḥ (slight aspiration of the preceding vowel)
h *h*im
i *i*n
ī s*ee*
j *j*et
jh aspirated j as in lo*dgeh*ouse (approx)
k *k*ill
kh aspirated k similar to kh in wor*kh*ouse
ḷ a short vowel resembling lry in reve*lry*
ḹ similar to ḷ, but longer. Usually not found in the text
l *l*ip
ṃ (nasalization of the preceding vowel)
m *m*eet
ṅ si*ng*
ṇ a*n*d
ñ ni*ñ*a (girl child) as in Spanish
n *n*ever
o no
p *p*en
ph aspirated p similar to ph in u*ph*ill

ṛ	short retroflex vowel slightly resembling short 'i' in the third syllable in *ability*
ṝ	similar to ṛ, but longer
r	*r*un, but more audible than in English resembling that in Italian
ś	*she*
ṣ	as in she but retroflex
s	*s*it
ṭ	*t*ip, but retroflex
t	wa*t*er, but dental
ṭh	aspirated ṭ similar to th in an*th*ill
th	aspirated t similar to th in *Th*ailand
u	p*u*t
ū	r*u*de
v	*v*ery
y	*y*es

1. Introduction

Absolutism is a broad philosophy which is based on the concept of "the absolute". The absolute is something which is eternal, unconditional, perfect, unchanging and self-sufficient. In religion God is often treated as the absolute. In western philosophies the will (Schopenhauer), intuition (Bergson) and ego (Fichte), etc. are considered the absolute by various philosophers.

Relativism or relativity is the opposite of absolutism. It is non-absolutism where a phonomenon is considered in relation to other phenomena. A phenomenon is connected and can be viewed from different angles.

In ordinary language relativism appears quite patently. Consider the following statements :

a. He is a brilliant student.

b. She is beautiful.

c. This train moves rather slowly.

d. India has made a lot of progress after Independence.

e. I find this novel absolutely boring.

In each of these statements there are adjectives and adverbs which are relative. For example, a student may be brilliant according to one standard, but average according to another. Your friend may find a novel boring while you may consider the same novel highly interesting. Similarly, the words "beautiful", "slowly", " a lot of progress" may be contested by lay persons as well as experts who hold different views and standards.

Laws in different countries provide many examples of relativism. For example, homosexuality is a crime in India while in some western countries it is allowed under certain conditions. Consensual sex between unmarried adult men and women is legal in many western countries and also in India, but it is a crime in some countries. In India and most British commonwealth countries the vehicular traffic flows according to the left hand rule, while in the U.S.A. and many other countries the right hand rule is followed. Thus what is an offence of the traffic law in one system is the right way in the other.

Social customs, conventions and mores offer many instances of relativism. A society may consider non-vegetarian food a taboo while another may consider it not only normal but even necessary. Even within the same social group, customs may vary from one subgroup to another and from one family to another.[1]

In Jaina philosophy non-absolutism has great importance. Relativism is one of the most important tenets in Jaina philosophy as well as religion. Jainas regard reality as multi-faceted and thus relative. An object, for example, has infinitely many attributes and can be viewed from different standpoints which provide only partial truths. This philosophy is reflected in two principles sometimes treated as synonymous; *anekāntavāda* (*anekānta* for "not one end") and *syādvāda* (literally, "The doctrine of somehow").

To distinguish philosophical and socio-cultural relativity from the relativity of Einstein's theory of relativity in physics, we will use the word "relativism" in the former case and reserve the word "relativity" in the context of the latter.

Einstein`s relativity theory is one of the two revolutionary theories in physics which were propounded in the early 20th century. The other is the quantum theory to which Einstein made a major contribution.

Einstein`s special theory was proposed in 1905 and his general theory appeared in 1915. The relativity theory demolished the earlier concepts of absolute space and absolute or universal time. In fact physicists preferred to speak of space-time instead of space and time which were intricately entangled with each other. The results of relativity theory may be briefly summarized :

1. Both space and time are relative, being related to various observers.
2. The velocity of electromagnetic radiation of which the visible light occupies a small range is constant for all observers.
3. Under certain circumstances mass gets converted into energy and vice versa.
4. In the presence of a gravitational field space-time becomes "curved". In other words the behavior of a body in space-time is modified depending on the pattern of the field.

We shall discuss relativity at some length later.

Relativity shook the very foundation of the basic concepts of physics, but its effect was not confined to physics alone. It was felt in almost all the branches of knowledge including philosophy, literature and popular science.

In a way it was unfortunate that Einstein used the name "relativity" for his theory. Since the words relative and relativity are extensively used in philosophy and most important in ordinary language, the theory gave rise to many misconceptions among lay persons as well as those who had studied science but were not familiar with relativity physics.

Some people began to say "everything is relative". Some others who were familiar with relativism in philosophy asserted, "Our ancient philosophers are vindicated". Some went even further. "Our philosophers had anticipated Einsteins's theory many centuries ago". Many science fiction writers indulged in such fantasies as "going back in time".

Jaina non-absolutism, as we pointed out earlier, is a philosophy of relativism with a well developed doctrine of *anekāntavāda* and *syādvāda*. It was quite natural for scholars in Jainism to liken these doctrines with relativity physics. A comparative analysis shows that there are similarities as well as differences between these two theories. What is true of Jaina relativism vis-a-vis relativity physics is also true to some extent of other relativistic philosophies.

It is not easy to compare Jaina theory with Einstein's theory. First, the former evolved in a socio-cultural milieu which is quite different from the modern scientific thought which shaped relativity physics. Second, this comparison can be facilated only through western logic, epistemology and ontology which differ from the concepts of Indian philosophy. We have to be particularly careful when we use western terminology while discussing Indian philosophy.

Relativism in philosophy is very broad and encompasses a huge mass of knowledge. Einstein's theory on the other hand is confined to a small area of physics and its author did not have any ambition to expand its scope. Nevertheless, we will briefly discuss towards the end how attempts have been made to integrate relativism and relativity theory.

2. Jainism

2.1 Mahāvīra

Jainism is one of the oldest religions of the world. Though its effective founder was Vardhamāna Mahāvīra (599 — 527 BCE) its elements can be traced to Pārśva (c 9th century BCE) about whom not much is known. Mahāvīra ("the great hero") is treated as the last or 24th *tirthaṅkāra* ("ford-maker"). Jainism symbolizes a rebellion against the caste system and animal sacrifice prevalent among Hindus. As religion and philosophy, Jainism is a heterodox system having no allegiance to the Vedas.

Like Gautama Buddha, Vardhamāna was born in a royal family and belonged to a martial clan. At the age of thirty he left his home leaving behind his wife and a daughter, in search of truth and liberation.

For about twelve years he was a wandering ascetic observing severe austerities, meditating and engaging in disputations. Initially he wore a single garment which he discarded later and lived in nudity. For some time he lived with his close friend Gośāla Maskarīpura.

Gośāla left him after a quarrel and founded a new sect of *Ājīvikas*. In the thirteenth year of asceticism he received complete enlightenment or *nirvāṇa*.

Jainism split into two sub-sects at the time of an exodus which took place at the end of Candragupta Maurya`s reign. The exodus was due to a famine. A large number of monks led by Bhadrabāhu went from the Ganges to the Deccan. Bhadrabāhu and his followers retained the rule of nudity while those who remained in the North led by Sthūlabhadra considered the use of white garments as permissible. The former sect is called *Digambaras* ("space-clad", i. e. naked) and the latter, *Śvetāmbaras* ("white-clad"). However, there is very little doctrinal difference between these sects.

Traditionally, oral sacred literature was transmitted down from the days of Mahāvīra. It is, however, believed that Bhadrabāhu was the last person to know it perfectly. After his death a great council was held at Pataliputra by Sthūlabhadra. The council approved a reconstructed version of the canon in the form of twelve *Aṅgas* or sections based on the earlier fourteen "former texts" (*Purvas*). This version was fully accepted by *Śvetāmbaras* and finally settled and written in Kathiawar in the 5th century CE. *Digambaras* seemed to have tried to produce their own literature, but much of it is still unpublished.

However, the texts are believed to have become corrupt and twelve *Upāṅgas* were added. During the Middle Ages many commentaries appeared in Prākrit as well as Sanskrit. Many Jaina monks contributed even to secular literature. For example, the famous poet Naycandra of the 14th century was a Jaina monk.

Jainism appeared prominent in the period between the Mauryas and Guptas from Orissa in the east to Mathura in the West. However, later it was mainly confined to Kathiawar Gujrat and some parts of Rajasthan. While, *Śventāmbaras* provailed here, *Digambaras* held sway in the former South Hyderabad and Mysore. Strangely Jainas influence waned considerably in the Ganges Valley, its original home.

Jainism gradually declined as Śaivism and Vaiṣṇavism grew. However, it did not disappear totally and today there are about three million Jainas in India.

It is interesting to note that Mahāvīra and Gautama Buddha (c 563 — 483 BCE) were contemporaries. There has always been interaction between their followers. This is the reason why Jainism and Buddhism have many common features.

2.2 Religion and Philosophy

Jainas are atheists who do not believe in a creator god. The world functions according to universal law. This leads to the philosophy of determinism. The universe is eternal but undergoes periodical cycles, each cycle producing twenty-four *tīrthaṅkāras*, twelve Universal Emperors (*cakravartins*) and sixty-three Great Men (*śalaka puruṣas*) at regular intervals. At the peak of the cycle people have enormous size and long life. They receive everything from wishing-trees (*kalpa-vṛkṣa*) and hence need no law or property. At the nadir of the cycle people become dwarfs with life expectancy of 20 years. The last *tīrthaṅkāra* in this cycle was Mahāvīra. At present we are in the declining phase in which religion will gradually wane and disappear. The declining phase is about 40,000 years of duration.

Jainsim recognizes five categories of non-living (*ajīva*) existents; "ether" (*ākāśa*), a secondary space (*dharma*) which allows movement, a tertiary space (*adharma*) which indicates means or condition of rest, time (*kāla*) and matter (*pudgala*)

These five categories along with *jīva* and *mokṣa* constitute seven fundamental categories (*tattvas*) in Jainism.[1]

Humans, animals, plants and even some entities such as rocks and running water have souls. Intrinsically, the soul is omniscient, bright and full of bliss. There are infinitely many souls in the world.

The soul is subject to the doctrine of *karma*.[2] However, unlike Hinduism and Buddhism, Jainas posit a material dimension to *karma*. It is represented by minute particles which adhere to the soul. Every activity good or bad occasions accumulation of *karma* on the soul. Evil actions entail heavier coating of *karma*. Depending upon the *karmic* clouding of the soul, the new locus of the soul is determined. The soul thus tranmigrates to another entity. This cycle of birth and death continues eternally unless a path to liberation is found. By abandoning action it is possible to reduce further accumulation of *karma*. Through penance *karma* can be annihilated. This method is called *nirjarā*. When liberated, the soul rises to the highest heaven where it remains blissful and inactive for ever. This is *nirvāṇa*. Needless to say those who aspire for liberation have to adopt an austere and disciplined life which incorporates penance to counter *karmic* effects. It is difficult to attain *nirvāṇa* for the lay person. Only monks can undergo such privations as giving up possessions including clothes, self-mortification, and a course of long study and meditation. In modern days it is believed that total liberation cannot be attained even by monks because complete renunciation requires living in nudity which is not followed even by *Digambaras* today.

One of the tenets of Jainism is non-violence (*ahiṃsā*). No living creature, however small or insignificant, should be harmed. Jaina monks usually wear nose-masks to prevent inhaling of insects. They may sweep the ground ahead of them so that they may not trample on insects. Some monks even refrain from washing their bodies lest they should kill lice and other parasites.

Jaina epistemology and ontology involve two basic principles. Jainas are empiricists. They may not reject "pure logic" (which in the West is deductive logic and laws of thought) because such logical exercise may motivate a person to investigate a problem further. But ultimately it is the empirical evidence which proves an assertion. However, empiricism should be interpreted in a broader sense to connote experience.

It appears that experiential revelations (say, through meditation) ratified by the peer group can lead to valid inferences. For example, the assertion of transmigration cannot be accepted by modern empiricists, but Jainas treat it as a verified principle.

The second doctrine relates to non-absolutism. Jainas believe that every object has countless attributes. Hence a statement relating to it made without mentioning contextual parameters is always incomplete. This has led to the doctrines of *syādvāda* and *anekāntavāda* which will be considered at some length later.

3. The Mind and Knowledge

3.1 The Mind

As mentioned earlier, Jainas are realists and empiricists. They believe in many-sided reality which can be congnized only through experience.

We gain experience through our perceptive organs and the mind. Jainism regards the mind as just an organ like eyes and ears. The function of the mind is to collate the sense data. Nevertheless, it is merely an instrument which discovers reality. It is not a creator of new facts, nor does it possess any innate or a priori knowledge. Unlike Kant in the West and Buddhist logicians Dignāga and Dharmakīrti, it does not regard categories and forms as mental phenomena.

Much discussion has taken place among various philosophical schools over the place of universals and particulars in the theory of knowledge. On the one extreme is the Platonic school which asserts that universals have real existence in a different dimension possibly in heaven, which are perfect archetypes of the class of the corresponding (imperfect) particulars such as cows, humans, etc. Plato also assumed that we had knowledge of these perfect prototypes before our birth. This is now called extreme realism. On the other end is the extreme nominalism of Roscelinus (1070 — 112 CE) who maintained that only particulars exist, universals are merely general terms used to designate particulars. The only thing real about the universal is the name. Aristotle stands in the middle of the spectrum; he regarded a universal as an essence which is revealed to us through our experience of particulars.

Jaina views are close to those of Aristotle. Jainas regard objects as possessing both universals and particulars. Every object thus is a particular and a universal rolled into one. What's more, acquaintance with a single object enables us to recognize another object as belonging to the same class. For example, if you see an elephant even once you can identify elephants later because the first elephant was a concrete universal.

Since according to Jainism the mind does not hold innate knowledge of "pure logic"; some misperceptions have ariesen in the minds of many philosophers. It is necessary to emphasize that though Jaina philosophy believes in empiricism and treats a priori logic as insufficient evidence of objectivity; it has no quarrel with the use of logic which is substantialted by empirical methods. It is quite intersting to investigate where the "laws of thought" which the western philosophers treat as innate to the human mind, and an invaluable epistemic tool, stand vis-a-vis Jaina epistemology.

3.2 Identity

These three Aristotelian laws of thought are the law of identity, the law of excluded middle and the law of contradiction.

The law of identity is usually accepted by all schools of philosophy but they are expressed in different forms :

1. If a proposition is true, it is true.
2. An object is equal to itself.
3. No two things are equal.
4. Every meaningful expression (concept, judgement, etc.) must be used in the same meaning.

Symbolically the law usually appears as A = A where ostensibly A can be anything, an object, a proposition, a set or a collection, an adjective, an adverb and so forth. However, the equality appears tautological and does not throw much light on the concept.

A better equation is A = B where the reference is not to the forms "A" and "B" but to their contents. The best interpretation possibly comes from Russell. The equation means that every proposition which is true of A is also true of B and vice versa.

Jainas cannot accept this law a priori and we need to discuss it with reference to experience. The first thing we need to observe is that a thing A never remains the same as time progresses. If you consider a motor car, it depreciates over time. At one moment it is stationary while at another moment it is running. At one moment it is at one place while at another moment it may be at another place. At a certain moment it may be carrying four passengers while at another moment it may carry two or three or just one person who drives the car. Its driver too may change from time to time. Its speed, fuel content, oil content, etc. may vary from time to time. Modern science tells us that we are all changing all the time, our cells are replaced periodically. The change becomes appreciable over a long time. For example, your friend Raman whom you last met twenty years ago would not have the same appearance today and you may even have some difficulty in recognizing him. However, the law of identity as expressed in terms of propositions remains valid because the various propositions can take care of all the variables (time, place, etc.) associated with the object whether a car or a person. A = B is valid at any given time.

Jainas go further than what is contemplated in A = B. For them, contradictories are closely related In fact, they cannot be separated. For example, a statement "a motor car exists" can be interpreted as "a motor car does not exist as a bicycle". If your car is in Mumbai it can be asserted that it is not in London. It would also be true that the car did not exist in 1805 CE. If the color of the car is black, it is false that the car is red or yellow. True to their doctrine of many sided viewpoints Jaina philosophers do not accept a statement as true or false without knowing the context.

Since Jainas treat different views to look at reality essential for complete knowledge and consider existence and non-existence as inseparable, it might be thought that they do not believe in the law of identity. It is true that they do not accept the law a priori, but their experience teaches them that there are some essential elements in an object which give it a unique status. Their view of an object as a universal concrete helps them identify an object in practice.

Suppose a Jaina philosopher meets his friend Milind after thirty years. The last time he saw him was when Milind was a young man in his twenties. Now in his fifties, Milind looks old, is thin and sports a beard. Nevertheless, the philosopher would recognize him, ableit with some difficulty, using his memory (which is a legitimate source of knowledge in Jainism).

In some cases Milind may have to identify himself by recalling his past assiciation with the philosopher. But once Milind is identified to his satisfaction, the philosopher will treat his friend as Milind in his future transactions with him. Though Milind has changed considerably, he remains Milind even for the philosopher.

Suppose you buy a car which you call Speedy. You have a close friend who is a Jaina philosopher and whom you call Phil who meets you quite often. The following is a brief biography of Speedy.

In the first five years Speedy runs well, is fuel efficient and requires only minor repairs apart from regular servicing Phil often refers to Speedy as an excellent car.

In the next five years Speedy begins to show signs of aging and fatigue. The fuel efficiency decreases, two of its glass windows are broken and other two do not function properly. The steering wheel does not work smoothly. The engine sometimes stops without any reason. The battery does not function properly. The tyres puncture very often. "Oh, your Speedy is getting old", remarks Phil.

At the end of ten years you decide to completely overhaul Speedy. The various systems are fitted with new parts wherever possible, the tyres are changed, the old upholstery is replaced by a new one giving the interior a better look. The windows are set right. An aircondintioner is installed. The car is painted again. The expenses are very high but the car looks like a new piece and there is considerable improvement in its working including fuel efficiencey. "Well, it looks as if you have bought a new car", says Phil "but I know it is the good old Speedy".

Speedy behaves extremely well for a year. However, the old troubles come back with greater vigor. Tyres puncture more often, the engine refuses to run more frequently. The gears, clutch and steering wheel become disfunctional almost every other day. Speedy has frequent breakdowns and has to be towed to the garage for extensive repairs where she remains idle for a long time. "Your Speedy is getting old. It is high time you sold the car", comments Phil.

You try to sell Speedy but there are no buyers to own an old model that falls sick often. You dismantle the car and start selling the parts at the best price available in the market. The engine is sold, so are some parts, including the battery and the tyres. The remaining parts lie scattered in your garage. Phil visits you one day. "Where is Speedy?", he asks. "Here" you say, pointing at the scattered junk. It takes some time for him to understand what has happened. "Oh, Speedy is no more", he laments, "she is dead".

This account shows that the philosopher had the unmistakable knowledge of what we call identity. This is because of his experience and acquaintance with Speedy's biography. He knew Speedy was not existent twenty years before. He knew she lived for about 14 years despite undergoing several inner and outer changes. He knew exactly when Speedy ceased to exist. Phil accepted that an object changes continuously, he accepted that every particular is accompanied by a universal, he also knew the functions of a car, the owner of Speedy and where it was registered. Though he may not agree, he knew what "carness" signifies. Throughout Speedy's life he had no doublts about her identity. And he had no doubt when the identity was lost for ever. The moral of this account is that Jaina philosophers do not accept the law of identity a priori, but their behaviour implies its validity under appropriate conditions.

3.3 Law of Contradiction

Classical western logic expresses this law as :

A cannot be both B and not-B. For example, a pencil cannot be yellow and not yellow simultaneously. An existent cannot be a tree and non-tree. A cannot both be and not be.

The truth of this law cannot be doubted. You may take this as an innate law of thought. You may also treat it as a linguistic fact in the sense the words "be" and "not be" are *ipso facto* incompatible. They cannot exist together because of the very construction of the words "be" and "not be" or "A and not A". If you look deeper you will find that the opposite characters of A and not-A are embedded in our experience. The Jaina view resembles this empirical argument.

However, Jainas emphasize the contextual factor. If you say the jar exists, without reference to place, time substance, etc. it may be misinterpreted. For example, if the jar exists in Paris, it does not exist in Chennai. If this jar exists qua jar it does not exist qua chair. The law of contradiction can be correct only when the entity is understood contextually. "If A is asserted to be existent, the assertion is significant only if it negates its nonexistence in its own context and implies its non-existence in a different context".[1]

An illustration would show how Jainas look at contradiction.

Suppose a rectangular sheet of paper is divided into two parts along the length. The upper half is painted red and the lower part is painted blue. Jainas (as well as Nayāyikas) will assert that the statement "the paper is red and blue", is true. A Buddhist would treat red and blue as numerically different and thus would deal with each portion of the paper separately. Jainas rely on experience and "the paper is red and blue", is veridical because they believe in the unity of two portions of the paper and their view apparently violates the law of contradiction. But when the context is clear, i.e. when the statement is more explicit in the form "The upper half of the paper is red and the lower half is blue", Jainas will immediately concur showing that they do not violate the law of contradiction.

3.4 Excluded Middle

The law of excluded can be expressed as :

A is either B or non-B

A proposition is true or false (not true)

Thus humans are either mortal or immortal. There is no third alternative, *tertium non datur*, i.e. “a third is not given”.

This law, again, appears quite natural as arising from innate logic of the mind or stemming from the very linguistic construction.

Some western logicians do not agree with this law. For example, According to Brower, truth can be defined only in terms of verifiability and propositions can be divided into three categories, viz.

1. Propositions which are verifiable.
2. Propositions whose contradictories are verifiable.
3. Propositions which are neither verifiable nor are their contradictories verifiable.

According to Brower a proposition falling in the third category is meaningless and the law is not applicable. But what is meant by verifiability? It means a proposition “can” (in theory) be verified. It does not mean that it is verified in practice.

Suppose it rains heavily on a small island of area 1 sq.km for a week. All the observed parts, central, coastal and middle have received rain. It would be churlish to ask whether a small unobserved part about one meter square near the centre of the island has received the rain because it was not actually observed. The meteorological records indicate that for the last hundred years all the observed parts (which include this particular area) of the island have received rain during this season. The contention that this small part did receive rain appears quite legitimate. At worst it did not receive any precipitation this time. But to deny that it “received or did not receive rain” is to make a mockery of how we use induction through repeated observation.

Moreover, if we do not accept this law we would not be able to assert that not-not-P = P. Hence most western logicians assume this law.

These three laws are claimed to be violated in some quantum phenomena, i.e. events which occur at subatomic level. We will discuss this aspect with special reference to *anekāntavāda* in a separate chapter.

We may conclude this chapter with a brief recap. Jaina philosophy is based on experience. It believes in multiple facets of reality and assumes every object can be predicated in infinitely many ways. It believes that every object is a concrete universal displaying a particular and universal These beliefs lead to the conclusion that it accepts all the three laws of thought in proper context. There are some scholars who believe that the law of middle is not accepted by Jainas because *anekāntavāda* consists of seven statements (*nayas*) which together constitute reality. This is in contrast to our bivalent logic (P or not-P)

However, this raises a question whether the seven-statement formula is a logical system in which the word logic means "pure logic". This will be discussed later. We may safely conclude that Jainas accept all the three laws when the context is clearly stated.

4. Non-absolutism or *Anekāntavāda*

4.1 *Saptabhaṅgī*

We have seen that Jainas regard reality as multifaceted. Every existent possesses infinitely many attributes. We have also noted that affirmation and negation are not separable. The complete knowledge of an object can be obtained instantaneously only by an omniscient *jina* such as Mahāvīra. For common people, Jainas have devised a system of *anekāntavāda* which is the theory of sevenfold predication. Thus the doctrine of non-absolutism or relativism is encompassed in a seven-step formula. Jainas contend that not only existence but any attribute can be completely defined in terms of this seven-sided system. Each one of these statements gives only a partial knowledge, while all the statements together give a complete view of reality.

This system is called *saptabhaṅgī* (sevenfold predication). *Anekāntavāda* is sometimes called *syādvāda*, but some scholars see them as distinct doctrines though their difference is minimal. This view is relevant in the evolution of *anekāntavāda*.

According to Malliṣeṇa, author of *Syādvādamañjarī* :

> The particle *syāt* signifies manifoldness. Therefore *syādvāda* is *anekāntavāda* the doctrine of manifoldness. And that means the acceptance of the view that a single entity is variagated by many and various attributes or properties (*dharma*), viz. eternal, non-eternal, etc.[1]

An example of *saptabhaṅgī* may be furnished. Every statement below contains the word *syāt* which may be translated as "from a certain point of view"

1. (*Syāt*) the pen exists.
2. (*Syāt*) the pen does not exist.
3. (*Syāt*) the pen exists and (*syāt*) does not exist.
4. (*Syāt*) the pen is indescribable (*avaktavya*)
5. (*Syāt*) the pen both exists and is indescribable.
6. (*Syāt*) the pen both does not exist and is indescribable.
7. (*Syāt*) the pen exists, does not exist and is also indescribable.

Each of these statements needs to be elucidated.

First Statement

This statement is with reference to the subject pen itself. The pen's existence is asserted by way of its intrinsic (*sva* -) properties and negated with reference to its alien (*para*-) properties. This is the reason why *syāt* is affixed which makes the statement contextual. Usually, substance (*dravya*), attribute (*bhāva*), time (*kāla*) and space (*kṣetra*) are believed to constitute the context, but you may add any other determinant which is relevant to the context.

Thus the first statement can be amplified as :

The pen exists as pen and not as chair.

This pen exists here in Delhi and not in London.

This pen exists now, but it did not exist five years ago.

This pen uses ink and not water to write.

This pen is owned by Ashok, not by Vinod, etc.

You may think some of the properties such as ownership are not intrinsic. For two reasons we can add any provisos. First, the four determinants mentioned earlier do not exhaust all possibilities of the context. Secondly, Jainas consider relations as intrinsic and not external, hence any relation, (e.g. ownership) which prevails in reality is relevant to the context.

Second Statement

In the second statement the pen's existence is with reference to another. It refers to either alien properties or is out of context. For example, the pen does not exist as pencil; it does not exist in Paris and so on.

We recall that Jainism regards opposites as inseparable. The pen is not only a pen, it is not not-pen. The very sentence "this is a pen" implies this is not A, B, C..., etc. If the first statement is used without *syāt*, an unconditional version "the pen exists" could be interpreted as "the pen exists in London".

Similarly the second unconditional statement "the pen does not exist", could be interpreted as "the pen does not exist in Delhi". Both statements do not agree with reality that the pen is in Delhi and Delhi only.

If it is understood that *syāt* in the first statement implies self-reference and *syāt* in the second implies alien reference (which is the opposite of the first), it means both these statements convey the same meaning. The question arises as to why two separate statements are required in such a case. Mookerjee offers an explanation. According to him the first statement rebuts unqualified existence and hence also rebuts absolute non-existence. This makes the existence determinate. In the same way, the second statement makes non-existence determinate by rebutting absolute non-existence and absolute existence. According to him each predicate precludes the operation of the opposite predicate.[2]

Third Statement

The third statement should be read with regard to the succession of the reference to itself and the reference to the alien.

A question now arises about the *raison d'etre* of the third statement. According to Mookerjee the third statement is different from the mere addition of the first two :

Suppose that a jar and a chair are successively perceived in a room and we assert the existence of the entities therein. But the two are not different from each one of them. If "two" is but a summation of the units, the third proposition is nothing but a summation of the first two. But the Jaina would appeal to experience. Take for instance the word "go". It is nothing but the successive occurances of two letters "g" and "o" . That the word "go" is different from both "g" or "o" is a matter of perception. If the distinctive unity of the word "go" were not a fact, and it were identical with constituent letters, the pronunciation of "g" and "o" would be sufficient for communicating the meaning of "go".[3]

However, Mookerjee's analogy does not appear to be convincing. In the case of the third statement there is a juxtaposition of two almost identical statements while in the above illustration, the individual constituents are mere letters, while their combination belongs to a different category; it is a word having meaning.

Fourth Statement

This must be understood with regard to the rererence to itself (first statement) and "simultaneity" of the reference to another (second statement).

"Inexpressible" is the translation of *avaktavya*. This seems to arise because of simultaneity of the first two statements involved in it. Consider the statement "there is a solar eclipse". This proposition is true under certain circumstances and false under other circumstances. *Avaktavya* springs up when one asserts the statement is both true and false simultaneously "in the same breath" under the same conditions.

According to Sāmantabhadra as well as Vidyānanda, the expression "true and false" (in succession) consists in gradual (*kramārpaṇa*) assignment of values "true" and "false" while the "inexpressible" arises from assigning these values simultaneously.[4]

The simultaneous pronouncements of opposites are believed to give rise to a connotaion in the fourth statement, which is different from that in the third.

Suppose you have a glass of water to which you add a spoonful of sugar and some lime juice. The resultant is neither pure water nor sugar nor lime juice, it may be treated as a sweet drink. Its constituents have lost their identities.

The fourth proposition is believed to arise because the simultaneous occurrence of opposite predicates cannot be expressed in one word and hence it is inexpressible.

Fifth Statement

This statement should be read with regard to reference to itself and simultaneity of reference to itself and reference to another.

In this statement there is compressence of two attributes, existence and inexpressibility.

Sixth Statement

The sixth statement is with regard to reference to the alien self and simultaneous reference to itself and another. There is thus compresence of non-existence and *avaktavya.*

Seventh Statement

This is with regard to reference to itself, reference to the alien self and simultaneity of reference to itself and to the alien.

Various commentators emphasize that *anekānavāda* is not the theory of indefiniteness of being as claimed by Jacobi, or non-equivocality as F.W. Thomas misperceives.[5] The theory does not imply indetermination or doubt or scepticism. It does not even suggest Buddhist agnosticism. Every proposition is relatively true. The whole septet (if such a term is permissible) reflects epistemic and ontologic reality though its components or individual statements may appear logically incorrect on surface.

It must be made clear that *saptabhangī* is true for any other pair of opposite attributes in addition to existence and non-existence.

For example,

1. (*Syāt*) the jar is red.
2. (*Syāt*) the jar is not red.
3. (*Syāt*) the jar is red and not red.
4. (*Syāt*) the jar is inexpressible.
5. (*Syāt*) the jar is red and inexpressible.
6. (*Syāt*) the jar is not red and is inexpressible.
7. (*Syāt*) the jar is red, not red and is inexressible.

Of course, these statements are subject to the same conditions and reference as explained in case of existence.

4.2 The Inexpressible

Unfortunately, it is not quite clear what *avaktavya* means. This can be interpreted as "inexpressible", "indescribable", "underterminable" or "indefinite" or even "uncertain". The following interpretations need to be taken into account seriously by those who stand by *saptabhaṅgī* philosophy.

(1) Mookerjee uses the word "indefinite" for *avaktavya*. He argues on the following lines : [6]

A real is a particular and a universal rolled into one. It is also true that being and not-being are both predicable of a real.

A real is thus existent, non-existent and is both existent and non-existent. But this view is not subjective but is based on objective attributes subject to some limitations.

The Third Statement conveys that existence and non-existence have a composite unity. The whole is identical with elements in one sense but is also different from the elements in another sense.

The fact, however, is that this togetherness of existence and non-existence when viewed simultaneously (Fourth statement) cannot be expressed in one word. The two opposite predicates can be asserted in succession, but the unity cannot be expressed by a single predicate. In this sense it is inexpressible. This applies to every real.

According to Bhartṛhari an expression is the essence of consciousness and hence of all that exists and whatever can be thought of is expressible. On the other hand Buddhists believe that a real is absolutely inexpressible. Unfortunately, this belief would lead to an absurd conclusion that verbal expressions have no bearing on reality. This is not acceptable to Jainas because it is contrary to experience.

Jainas take the middle way; a real is not totally expressible nor is it totally inexpressible. A real being amenable to different predicates is expressible as well as inexpressible. Since a real has both characteristics of being and not being, its state cannot be expressed in one word. It is in this sense that a real is inexpressible. Mookerjee endorses Vimaladāsa's solution : [7]

The word *avaktavya* is a negative term and has no positive significance. It simply asserts that the real *qua* possessed of existence and non-existence as attributes is not capable of being expressed by a word as no word can have such a double sense.

(2) Some western scholars have interpreted *saptabhaṅgī* as a system of logical alternatives and tried to incorporate *avaktavya* into a many valued logical system. It is tempting to assign *avaktavya* a third value (uncertain, indefinite, underteminable, etc.) in addition to two truth values of "true" and "false" in the bivalent system. However, Jaina scholars remind us repeatedly that *avaktavya* does not mean uncertain or indeterminate. This is discussed in a later chapter.

(3) The *saptabhaṅgī* septet is valid for every predicate. It is a general philosophy of standpoints. What is the place of discovery in this tenet? Suppose a Jaina philosopher in the tenth century were to see a mobile phone and its working. This is only an imaginary scenario for illustration – he would find the mobile and its working strange. If he calls it inexpressible he has a clue as to how he should proceed to investigate the matter. This "inexpressible" is

not the "inexpressible" in the Fourth Statement. At the most, he may treat this as the subject and use it in the septet as follows:

The inexpressible exists.

The inexpressible does not exist.

The inexressible exists and does not exist.

The inexpressible is inexpressible ...

and so on.

There is no extra knowledge he gains from this exercise. In other words, though Jainas swear by empiricism, *anekāntavāda* does not provide them the tools for a new discovery. But we cannot blame medieval Jaina scholars, for they lived in pre-scientific days. But this is an aspect to be remembered when Jaina relativism is compared with relativity physics.

Of course, in the above case the inexpressible leads to an endless regress. This will be discussed shortly.

(4) In light of what we said in (3), a question arises as to whether the Fourth Statement has a definite meaning. Consider:

The jar is indescribable.

It was earlier mentioned that, this view is based on simultaneity of existence and non-existence. Since the fact cannot be indicated by one word, the "indescribable" was used. But this leads to a paradox. Suppose the jar is indescribable which means it cannot be predicated by one word, but "indescribable" is the word we have used, hence contradication. Conversely, suppose the jar is expressible or describable. This contradicts the very statement, viz. the jar is indescribable.

The paradox can be resolved if we realize that the word "inexressible" belongs to a higher "logical type" than the words "exists". "is blue", etc. In other words, it is metalinguistic. Discussion of this topic is beyond the scope of this book. But there is one way of removing the paradox. The assertion "simultaneity of existence and non-existence cannot be predicated by one word" should be replaced by "simultaneity of existence and non-existence cannot be predicated by one word except 'indescribable' or 'inexressible' or its equivalent".

(5) An object or its attribute may be inexpressible because the person's senses are abnormal. He may suffer from jaundice or be introxicated or mentally disturbed and is the victim of illusion or delusions. His observation of the object being inexpressible is not subject to *saptabhaṅgī* because the Fourth Statement is valid for all attributes which are not subjective. This though true, suggests that *saptabhaṅgī* is purely a philosophical system in which "inexressible" does not lead to further scientific discovery, (e.g. investigation of the cause of inexressibility)

(6) The fifth, sixth and seventh statements are combinations of the first four statements. Each of them involves the *avyaktavya* and the first three. For example, in the fifth existence with reference to itself is juxtaposed with the *avyaktavya*. It possibly means a standpoint in which the object's own existence is more dominant than the existence of another.

In his paper "Anekanta : Both yes and no" B. K. Matilal rightly points out that given three alternatives yes (+), no (-) and inexpressible (0), the septet shows all possible combinations +, -, + -, 0, 0 +, 0 -, 0 + -

Indians have always shown a great penchant for permutations and combinations. In Karnataki music, the 17th century musician Vyankatamukhi created 72 *thāṭas* based on all possible combinations from the two blocks of notes, each block containing all possible variants of the seven notes of the *saptaka*. I have called this pattern in rituals "pattern completion".[8]

In the present case, we can consider two "operations", viz. "succession" (x) and "simultaneity" (y). +, -, 0 can be called elements We can arrange these three elements with two operations as follows :

One element : +, -, 0

Two elements : + x -, 0 x +, 0 x -, 0 y +, 0 y –

Three elements : 0 x + x -, (0 y +) x -, (0 x +) y -, o y + y–.

We have assumed that simultaneity prevails over succession. We have assumed some operations insignificant and commutative and associative properties of a single operation, viz. ab = ba, a (bc) = (ab) c. We arrive at 12 combinations or *nayas*. Again, by relaxing some assumptions (e.g. treat 0 x + different from + x 0) we can further increase the number of steps.[9]

However, Jainas insist that there are seven and only seven combinations. Any reduction would make the system incomplete and any addition would make some steps redundant.

(7) V. Venkatachalam in his paper "The Seven-Plank Epistemological Frame — A Search for its Rationale" [10] makes a few interesting suggestions. His *saptabhaṅgī* is based on seven types of experience; *pramā* (valid experience), *vikalpa* which projects *asattva*, *saṃśaya* (doubt) and four types of *brhama* or *mithyājñāna*.[10] Steps 4 - 7 are quite interesting.

In the fourth step *avyaktavya)* is treated as *nirupādhika brhama* similar to that found in the roap being mistaken for the snake.

The remaining three steps are treated as *sopādhika brhamas*.

In the fifth step, the *brhama* is qualified by *sattva* (reality). For example, when one sees two moons while in reality there is only one. In the sixth step the *brhama* is qualified by *asattva* (unreality), e.g. when the illusion of horse in the picture co-exists with the full realization of the unreality of a horse. In the seventh the *brhama* is qualified by both reality and unreality in the experience. For instance, the case when "the jaundiced eye witnesses the reality of the yellowness in the conch simultaneously with the conviction of unreality of the yellowness on the basis of the strong *saṃskāra* of previous experience of the same conch at home."[11]

Unfortunately, Venkatachalam's suggestions appear to contradict a basic principle of *saptabhaṅgī*. Jaina philosophers repeatedly tell us that the seven standpoints are applicable to any predicate. This means every experience leads to seven different views. Venkatachalam, on the other hand, associates a different view with each distinct exerience. However, his views constitute an attempt to bring *anekānta* in line with modern thinking. Nevertheless, he sticks to the seven-step formula. In a later chapter I have discussed how *anekānta* can be enriched especially in the light of modern science.

5. *Syādvāda* and *Nayavāda*

5.1 *Syādvāda*

Syādvāda though equated with *anekāntavāda* in the form of *saptabhaṅgī* is believed by some scholars to be slightly different from it for historical reasons.

Mahāvīra mentions two types of knowledge in Āgama texts, *pramāṇa* and *naya*. While the word *siyā* appears as a qualifier, there is no mention of *syādvāda* or the seven-fold formula.

Umāsvāti in his *Tattvārthādhigamasūtra* states that knowledge is obtainable by means of *pramāṇa* and *naya*, but does not use the word *syādvāda*.

Kundakunda (c 3 — 4 cent. CE), too, does not mention *syādvāda*, but in his *Pavayaṇasāra* the seven-fold formula is explicit.[1]

Siddhasena Divākara (c 6 — 7 cent. CE) is believed to be the first author to use the term *syādvāda*. In his *Nāyāvatāra* he observes:

> Object of Omniscient knowledge is composed of infinite attributes, while that of *naya* (knowledge based on a particular standpoint) consists of a single aspect. And since the *naya* rolling on the course of the scriptural knowledge (*śruta*), determines the partial aspect of object, the knowledge which asertains the whole aspect of object is called *syādvāda-sūtra*.[2]

Samantabhadra (c 600 CE) in his *Āptamimāṃsā* elucidates many conceptions. *Syādvāda* is the assertion by some way or other (*kathaṃcit*) by discarding absolutism in every resect. It depends on a seven-fold formula, viz. *saptabhaṅga* and view-point (*naya*). It tells us what to accept and what to reject. According to him the right knowledge (*pramāṇa*) of reality is of two types; one reveals the whole aspect of an object simultaneously, while the other does it successively, i.e. through *syādvāda* and *naya*. The right knowledge can also be revealed intuitively. It is called omniscient knowledge (*kevala jnāna*). Any knowledge other than these two types is false knowledge. He divides even absolute view (*ekānta*) into two types; (1) false absolutism (*mithyaikānta*) which accepts one particular aspect only, (2) true absolutism (*samyag-ekānta*) which adheres to one aspect without rejecting the other, each representing *naya* and *durnaya* respectively.

However, he explicitly mentions that the right knowledge (*pramāṇa*) should be qualified by the term *syāt*. This is precisely non-absolutism or *anekāntavāda*.

Akalaṅka Deva (c 720 — 780 CE) whom Uno considers as the first scholar to systematize Jaina logic and philosophy, divides the forms of *śrutra* (verbal and scriptural knowledge) into three groups; *durnaya, naya* and *syādvāda. Naya* is an incomplete and a partial expression (*vikalādeśa*), *syādvāda* is a complete expression (*sakalādeśa*). *Durnaya*, of course, is false knowledge. He specifically mentions that *syādvāda* consists of seven formulas considered from two opposite points of view, affirmation and negation. Akalaṅka speaks of three kinds of scriptural knowledge (*śruta*); (1) that which is derived from one's own perception according to other's indication (*pratyakṣa -nimittaka*) (2) that which is obtained from one's own reasoning (*anumāna nimittaka*), and (3) that which is produced by scripture (*āgama-nimittaka*). Akalaṅka's interpretation encompasses a wider area in contrast to the other commentators such as Vādideva who define *āgama* or *śruta* as cognition derived from the words of a reliable person (*āpta-vacana*)[3].

Vādideva Suri (1086 — 1169 CE) made a compendium of Jaina logic. *Pramāṇa nayatattvāloka*. He recognizes the types of knowledge, direct (*pratyakṣa*) and indirect (*parokṣa*). Direct knowledge involves awareness of an object (*avagraha*), speculation (īhā), perceptual judgement (*avāya*), retention (*dhāraṇā*), clairvoyance (*avadhi*) and telepathy (*manaḥparyāya*). Indirect knowledge consists of recollection (*smaraṇa*), recognition (*pratyabhijñāna*), knowledge leading to the cognition of invariable concomitance of probans with probandum (*tarka, ūha*), inference (*anumāna*) and scriptural knowledge (*āgama*)

5.2 Malliṣeṇa

Modern commentators consider Hemacandra, Siddhasena Divākara, Vādideva Suri and Malliṣeṇa as extremely important Medieval sources of Jaina philosophy. According to Uno, Malliṣeṇa's interpretation is mainly based on the three verses of *Vitarāgastuti* (VS). These verses are:

Entity when taken in its entirety, is without mode, and when taken in its part, it is without substance. You have seen fully the truth composed of seven formulas (modes) according to the distinction of expression - the truth which is knowable only by the typical wise (VS XXIII)

"Non-existence", "existence" and "inexpressibility" in an entity are not contradicted, when accompanied by different conditions. Without this understanding, the stupid, afraid of contradiction fall slain by the view of non-absolutism. (*anekānta-vāda*). (VS XXIV)

In some respect, an entity is perishable and eternal; similar and dissimilar; expressible and inexpressible; existent and non-existent. Oh Master of the wise! This is the succession of eructations which follow upon the nector of deep-drunk truth (VS XXV)[4].

According to Malliṣena, there are two kinds of *saptabhaṅgī*, viz. *saptabhaṅgī - pramāna*, and *saptabhaṅgī - naya*. The former pertains to *syādvāda* of seven statements, the latter pertains to *naya* (standpoints) of seven types starting with *naigama*, etc.

We have already discussed the first type earlier. The second type needs to be considered.

5.3 *Nayavāda*

The doctrine of nayavāda, too, is based on seven standpoints.

1. *Naigama* (the common) : In this method an entity's generic and specific qualities are not distinguished. Both the universal (*sāmānya*) and particular (*viśeṣa*) are recognized, but are treated as if each were absolute.
2. *Saṃgraha* (the general) : This viewpoint ignores the particular and mentions the general (*sāmānya*)
3. Vyavahāra (the practical) : This projects the view of common people.
4. *Ṛju-sūtra* : This view is based on the assertion that "the modification exists". It refers to the changing entity rather than its substance (*dravya*)
5. *Śabda* (the verbal) : This view acknowledges differences of connotations of synonyms related to gender, number, etc.

6. *Samabhirūddha* (the subtle) : This view recognizes subtle differences in the meanings of synonyms based on their etymologies, though they may have the same gender, number, etc.
7. *Evambhūta* : This viewpoint is based on the fact that a thing has an epithet only when it performs some act (*kriyā*) and not otherwise.

The following illustrations will elucidate the point :

1. A mango tree may be treated simultaneously as an individual having a definite size and shape and as a member of the species "mango tree".
2. It may be treated as a representative of the universal contained in the class "mango tree" ignoring its individual characteristics.
3. It may be considered merely as an individual.
4. It may be viewed from its present status as "bearing ripe mangos" irrespective of its past and future stages.
5. We may look upon an object from the viewpoint of its all synonyms recognizing their connotational differences as regards gender, number, etc., e.g. *kalatram, dārāh, patni*.
6. For the given gender and number, etc. the viewpoint may be shaped on the basis of etymology, e.g. Indra, Śakra, Purandara.
7. An actor may be called Hamlet when he plays the role of Hamlet in the Shakespear's play. But this epithet is only temporary.

The first three *nayas* which pertain to the object itself are called *dravyārthika*; the latter four deal with modifications and are called *paryāyārthika*.

It may be noted that *saptabhaṅgī-naya* and *saptabhaṅgī-pramāṇa* both have seven statements, but there is very little correspondence between the respective statements. Their only common feature is that their statements represent different views or standpoints.

Modern commentators have tried to explain why saptabhaṅgī-pramāṇa should contain seven and only seven propositions from the logical point of view but their argument does not seem to be convincing. They argue that the seven-fold pattern is applicable even to other opposites such as universality (*sāmānya*) and particularity (*viśeṣa*), transience (*nāśitva*) and perpetuality (*nityatva*), etc. But this demonstration is based on the premise of seven *bhaṅgas*; it does not explain why seven propositions are necessary and sufficient.

There is a motivational (generative) explanation. It is assumed that a character of an object (*vastu-dharma*) gives rise to seven doubts (*saṃdeha*). These seven doubts lead to seven curiosities (*jijñāsā*). These in turn give rise to seven questions (*paryanuyoga*) whence appear seven propositions.

One is tempted to believe that the number seven has become unnecessarily sacrosanct, and generations of commentators have clinged to it as an inviolable principle that correctly embodies infinitely many attributes. With a little ingenuity the number of propositions can be increased.

5.4 Synthesis and Analysis

Pramāṇa-vākya is defined as a complete statement that simultaneously expresses an entity having infinitely many natures through right knowledge (*pramāṇa*) by emphasizing existences as a unity. There is a holistic approach to the entity keeping in mind different deteterminants, time, nature, etc.

In other words, distinctions are eclipsed by a non-distinct composite view. One may say that all attributes are identified with their locus (*dharmin*). On the other hand, a partial statement (*naya vākya*) is one in which primary emphasis is on the distinction. It expresses in succession the attributes of an entity such as a pot which is known from a particular point of view.[5]

Thus *saptabhaṅgī-pramāṇa* is a septet which is a complete statement (*sakalādeśa*) based on the *pramāṇa-vākya*, while *saptabhangī-naya* is a partial statement (*vikalādeśa*) that represents a set of propositions based on particular points of view. It seems there is no unanimity as to which septet constitutes *naya-vāda* : (1) *Saptabhaṅgī-naya* mentioned here or (2) seven-fold formula with naigama, etc. mentioned in section 5.3.

According to Uno the difference between the two statements *saptabhṅgī-pramāna* and *saptabhṅgī-naya* is as follows :

1. In the former the whole entity is comprehended synthetically while in the latter a real is analyzed taking its attributes successively.
2. In the former non-distinction (*abheda-vṛtti*) is emphasized while in the latter, difference (*bheda - vṛtti*) is highlighted.
3. The former depends on right knowledge, while the latter on particular points of view (*naya*).

It is interesting to see how "with simultaneity" (*yaugapadyena*) and "in succession" can be viewed in the light of *abheda-vṛtti* and *beheda-vṛtti*. When such attributes as existence are treated as "distinct" relative to determinant like time, etc. one word is insufficient to express countless attributes in the same breath, hence the term "in succession" is used.[6] When own forms of these infinitely many attributes are projected as non-distinct with respect to time, etc. "even a term, say *asti* signifying a single attribute existence is capable of expressing an entity possessed of that attribute and remaining ones, in virtue of its implication. Thus the term 'with simultaneity' is employed".[7]

Earlier we mentioned four main contextual determinants. Uno mentions eight, viz. time (*kāla*), nature (*ātmarūpa*), entity (*guṇin, artha*, locus of attribute), relation (*saṃbandha*), service (*upakāra*), locality of the entity (*guṇi-deśa*), contact (*saṃsarga*) and word (*śabda*).

A few illustrations will elucidate the significance of *abhedavṛtti* with respect to some determinants.

Time - Suppose "the jar exists" is the first proposition of *syādvāda*. The time when existence of the jar is cognized, then and only then all other attributes abide in the entity. Thus the attributes are non-distinct by time.

Relation - Existence is inherent in the jar and hence be treated as identical with it. All other attributes coextensively abide in the jar when they are considered non-distinct.

Locality - If the jar is in Moscow its existence abides there and all attributes when considered non-distinct also abide there.

There is no doubt that the list of these eight determinants is merely illustrative and not exhaustive. The list can be expanded without much difficulty.

According to Uno such *abhedavṛtti* is possible when noumenal point of view (*dravyārthika - naya*) is held as primary and phenomenal viewpoint (*paryāyārthika-naya*) is considered secondary. Conversely, when the phenomenal viewpoint is considered primary, *abhedavṛtti* cannot be considered because the several attributes appear distinct.

We do not pursue this discussion on *bheda-vṛtti* and *abheda-vṛtti* further since scholarly opinions differ and the subject tends to appear confusing.

5.5 Criticism of *Syādvāda*

Syādvāda and *anekānta* have been adversely criticized by the adherents of orthodox *darśanas* and western scholars. Most criticisms are invalid because they are based on premises not assumed by Jainas. Those philosophies which are based on other premises would naturally find fallacies in *saptabhaṅgī* and the doctrine of *syādvāda*. A few criticisms are mentioned below.

1. Universality and paricularity are opposite attributes and hence they cannot exist concurrently in the entity in the same way that an object cannot be both hot and cold. This is the fallacy of contradiction (*virodha*). Its refutation is simple. Universality and particularity are not opposite. Every entity is a universal and a particular rolled into one.
2. The locus of affirmation cannot be the locus of negation. This is the fallacy of non-existence (*vaiyadhi-karaṇya*). This can be refuted by pointing out that the existence is with reference to the nature of the entity itself while assertion of non-existence is with reference to an alien nature.
3. When a thing is universal from one aspect, say, *svarūpa* and particular from another aspect, say, *pararūpa*, both aspects are correlative due either to one nature or to double nature, viz. *astitva* and *nāstitva*.[8] In the former the fallacy of non-coexistence remains *status quo*, while the latter consists of *astitva* and *nāstitva* and hence each of these two natures will be required for each of the two natures and so on *ad infinitum*. This is the fallacy of endless regress. Here the rebuttal is easy : both the universal and

particular are revealed in the same entity The question of *svarūpa* and *pararūpa* is irrelevant.

4. The fallacy of confusion occurs because an entity which is the locus of universality is also the locus of universality and particularity. Similarly the locus of particularity is also the combined locus of particularity and universality. Hence, the fallacy of confusion. The objection is based on the wrong schism between particularity and universality. (See 1 above). The objection is therefore erroneous.
5. There is an exchange of function and attributes; the aspect in which existence is asserted, the non-existence is affirmed and vice versa. This is the fallacy of transfusion. This argument can be easily rebutted by pointing out that existence and non-existence are in relation to different contexts.
6. The fallacy of doubt arises because there is no clear criterion to distinguish between existence and non-existence. Its rebuttal is that Jainas believe in the doctrine of non-absolutism and the fact that an object has infinitely many attributes. Hence a single criterion cannot be established for its existence and nonexistence.
7. There is a fallacy of non-determination flowing from (6). This fallacy is only apparent. Determination cannot be encompassed in a single word when there are countless attributes.
8. There is also the fallacy of renouncement of determination of subjective reality based on the fallacy in (6). Here the defence would be that *anekāntavāda* ultimately rests on empirical verification and a subjective reality has to be tested by objective evidence.

6. Jainism and Buddhism

6.1 Early Interaction

Mahāvīra and Gautama Buddha were contemporaries. Jainism and Buddhism have a common ground; they are both unorthodox religions and philosophical schools that do not owe allegiance to the Vedas unlike other *darśanas*. In fact Buddhism, too, incorporates relativism, though in a sense different from Jainas' concept. Buddhists consider two realities, phenomenal and the ulṭimate. Moreover, according to Nāgārjuna, the doctrine of *śunyatā* is also a philosophy of relativism, though many scholars have the misconception that *śūnyavāda* is nihilism.

Buddhist and Jaina philosophers have interacted with each other over many centuries with the result that notwithstanding their disputes, they seem to have borrowed much from their perceived rivals.

Pali literature in earlier days contains rudiments of *anekāntavāda* and its two wings *syādvāda* and *nayavāda*. Some insight can be gained through this literature on the development of Jaina non-absolutism.

Gautama is believed to have responded to a question in four ways.

1. Categorical answer (*ekaṃsa -vyākaraṇīya*)
2. Posing a counter-question (*paṭipucchāvyākarṇīya*)
3. Question is set aside (*ṭhāpaṇīya*)

4. Answer through analysis (*vibhājjavyākaraṇīya*)[1]. He claimed that he was *vibhājjavādin*. Jainas' *Sūtrakṛtāṅg* too exhorts Jaina monks to explain a problem using the technique of *vibhājjavāda*. This shows that Buddhists and Jainas followed the method of analysis.

Jain conjectures that the above method gradually gave rise to *ekaṃsavyākarṇīya pañhā* and *anekaṃsavyākaraṇiya pañhā* which correspond to Jaina *ekaṃsikā dhammā* and *anekaṃsikā dhammā*. Later the second class seems to have been divided into *vibhājjavyakaraṇīya* and *ṭhāpaṇīya*.[2]

In his preachings, Gautama Buddha used *anekaṃsikā* which is similar to Jaina *anekāntavāda*. However, "Jainism accepts all statements to possess some relative (*anekānta*) truth, while Buddhism does not accept that all non-categorical statements (*anekaṃsikā*) can be true or false from one standpoint or another. *Anekāntavāda* unlike *anekaṃsika-vāda* conceives of the possibility of knowing reality from one or more standpoints".[3]

In the course of addressing kalāmās, Gautama mentions ten possible methods of claiming knowledge. One of them is *nayahetu*. *Naya* is a method of statement which lends a meaning to a particular judgement. *Jātaka* points out that the wise man draws a particular standpoint. Since Jainas use *naya* in the same sense, B. Jain conjectures that the *nayahetu* of Buddhism was borrowed from Jainism. Jainas' *sunaya* and *durnaya* too have found a place in Buddhist philosophy. He also maintains that Buddhist concept of *paccekasacca* (partial truth) has also been influenced by Jaina *nayavāda*.[4]

6.2 *Syādvāda*

According to B. Jain the conception of *syādvāda* originated in Jainism which is considered the oldest surviving Indic religion. *Syādvāda* found its way into Vedic and Buddhist religions.

The first four propositions of *syādvāda* viz. *syādasti, syānnāsti, syādastināsti* and *syādavaktavya* are sometimes traced to the school of sceptics headed by Sañjaya Belaṭṭhiputta. Their fourfold formula resembles the first four statements of *syādvāda*. This view, however, is contested by such scholars as Jacobi.

Makkhali Gosāla, the founder of Ājīvika sect is also believed to have contributed to the development of *syādvāda* concept. According to Basham, Ājīvikas accepted the epistemology of Jainas "without going to the over-refined extreme of *saptabhaṅgī*, as in the orthodox Jaina *syādvāda*".[5] Their three-statement scheme is simpler than the four-step formula of sceptics and the seven-step formula of *syādvāda*. It is called *trirāśis.*

This is reflected in Dīghanakha's account :

1. I agree with all views.
2. I agree with no views.
3. I agree with some views and disagree with other views.[6]

These three statements resemble the first three *bhaṅgas* of *saptabhaṅgī* viz. *syādasti, syānnāsti* and *syādasti-nāsti*. This may be the intermediate stage of *syādvāda*. Gautama Buddha favoured a four-fold formula :

1. It is (*atthi*)
2. It is not (*natthi*)
3. It is and it is not (*atthi ca natthi ca*)

4. It neither is, nor is not (*na ca atthi na ca natthi*)

According to Miyamoto, Jaina *saptabhaṅgī* is equivalent to the above quartet : the first three predications correspond to the first three bhaṅgas while the fourth is equated with the next four propositions of *saptabhaṅgī* put together. According to B. Jain, however, the Buddhist quartet corresponds to the first four propositions of the Jaina septet. Jainas seem to have added the fifth, sixth and seventh propositions.

B. Jain points out that there is a difference between the Buddhist quartet and Jaina septet :

According to the Jaina scheme, all seven propositions could be true from relative standpoints, while in the Buddhist scheme only one proposition could be true. The propositions are not considered logical alternatives as considered in Buddhism.[7]

While interaction between Buddhists and Jainas cannot be doubted, the question as to who was the original author of a particular concept and who was its recipient has led to many controversies.

6.3 *Catuṣkoṭi*

The four-fold logic of Buddhists mentioned above may be expressed as:

1. A, 2. not A, 3. A and not-A, 4. Neither A nor not A.

Actually *catuṣkoṭi* literally means four extremes. The Buddhist Middle Way teaches avoidance of extremes. These extremes can be expressed in many quadrilemmas such as

a. Existence (*asti, bhāva, sat*)

b. Nonexistence (*nāsti, abhāva, asat*)

c. Existence and nonexistence (*sadasat, bhāvābhāva*)

d. Neither existence nor nonexistence (*naivāsti, na ca nāasti*)

Meaning of *Koṭis*

First Koṭi : A exists

This reflects the viewpoint of the common person who perceives a thing without further analysis. To some extent it resembles naive realism. A philosopher, too, may wrongly believe that the ultimate element in analysis is also the ultimate reality. Such people cling to the affirmative "A exists". They are the followers of eternalism.

Second Koṭi : A does not exist

Here a person clings to the view point "A does not exist". For her even a temporary cessation means nonexistence. This is called *annihilationism* or *nihilism*. Nāgārjuna even places the Vaipulyaka, one who clings to *śūnyatā* in the same category.

Third Koṭi : A exists and does not exist

There are some scholars who believe in this apparently self-contradictory statement. Their motive is to bring about syncretism.

Fourth Koṭi : A neither exists nor exists not

This fourth extreme view is equivalent to total denial. According to Ś*āstra*, "it is a fool's talk."[8]

However, K. Venkata has analyzed the third and fourth *koṭi* at length. According to him unlike Jainas, Buddhists despite being agnostic prefer to discuss transcendental dimension which appears in the last two *koṭis*. This has led to many schools of interpretations.

According to him, these four statements should be read in the spirit of the middle way; extremes should be avoided. "The alternative statements are different from extremes, precisely because the former are specific judgements made with the unmistakable awareness of other possibilities from other standpoints and their reflective judgements are pertinent to the mundane truth, the level of the relative."[9]

The four-step formula does not show clinging. These four propositions become mere alternatives or possibilities : each of them is true and all are true. For example, the ring finger is both long and short from different standpoints.

The above interpretations where clinging vitiates the import of the statements hold good for mundane facts. When one discusses the transcendental, the statements "is and is not", "neither is nor is not" are not false but irrelevant.[10]

Catuskoṭi affords exploration of knowledge at two different levels. First, at the conscious level, conventions help us to determine whether the propositional connection is valid or invalid on the basis of appropriate linkage of the universal (e.g. "whatever is a product is impermanent") with its reference (e.g. a vocal word). Second, at the subliminal level where one's consciousness is decoupled from logic and language, " no singular propositional linkage is ascertained, precisely because what is not there in convention A is accompanied by – A relating to the loss of referential existence".[11] This assertion will appear lucid if we realize that Buddhists consider a name A as always accompanied by its negative –A consciously or unconsciously. Language is a system consisting of symbols governed by semantic and syntactic rules. As Ichimura rightly observes, "Functionally naming an object by a symbol is referential, and linking another symbol to it is tendentious or purposive."[12]

Thus there appear to be two levels of validity; one dependent on convention (*vyavahāra*) and the second is insight (*paramārtha*). Nāgārjuna in Mādyamikaśastra says :

In teaching the doctrine (*dharma*) the Enlightened ones rely on the two truths, empirical (*vyavahāra or saṃṛtisatya*) and transcendental (*paramārtha satya*). Those who do not differentiate these two truths do not understand the profound reality (*tattva*) in the doctrine of the Buddha. Without relying on the empirical truth the transcendental truth cannot be shown; without relying on the transcendental truth, the *nirvāṇa* cannot be realized.[13]

The insight that both these truths need be understood is called *dvaya-satya*. However, Buddhists do not consider these two realms of truth totally independent; their relationship is best described dialectically as simultaneously identical (immanent) and different (transcendental) or "neither identical nor different". Most Buddhists seem to accept these two alternatives which characterize the unconventional *catuṣkoṭi*.

It is necessary to understand that ambiguity seems to be central to *catuṣkoṭi*. Nāgārjuna in *Madhyamakakārikāśāstra* maintains that despite the fact that from the point of view of conventional truth (*vyavahāratas*) the realms of *saṃsāra* and *nirvāṇa* ought to be clearly distinguished. However, he declares that (from the point of view of transcendental truth or *paramarthas*) no such distinction exists.[14]

According to Nāgārgjuna's thinking, the *pratyakṣa* which is nondualistic (*nirvikalpa*) activates the mind to create the semblance of two opposite correlates such as light and dark.[15]

It seems, of the pair, the mind selects the dominating element for assertion, negating the other, (e.g. asserting dark and negating light or vice versa).

Unlike Jainas Buddists maintain that existence and non-existence could be found simultaneously at the same locus. Jainas on the other hand view the world as the common person does. As we have already seen their interpretation of the compresence of existence and nonexistence is based on standpoints and the common person does not find any contradiction in it.

6.4 Relations and Causation

Buddhists posit at least two realities, the phenomenal world and the ultimate reality. The phenomenal events are mere projections of momentary point instants in the ultimate reality. In fact there are many series of momentary instants. These instants are disconnected The Buddhist doctrine of Dependent Origination suggests that a point instant depends on all previous point instants. However, Buddhists do not use the term "cause". Each point itself is an efficient moment and hence cause itself. This has led to the notion of functional dependence.

Buddhists thus live with a paradox, viz. moments appear in accordance with the causal law according to the doctrine of Dependent Origination, but they should be treated as just emerging according to a functional formula and not as "caused" in the usual sense of the term.

It is necessary to remember that these moments are translated into the phenomenal world as images again by a functional relationship.[16]

Jainas believe in empiricism and not in abstract logic. According to them, relations are objective verities, but a relation has no objective status outside the terms. They assume that relations come about as a result of internal changes in the nature of an existent.

We have seen the Buddhist dilemma which makes them avoid the word cause and speak instead of functional relationship. Jainas maintain that for causation to exist neither synchronism nor succession of related terms is necessary. As Mookerjee points out : Causality is a relation of determination. The effect is that whose coming into being is necessarily determined by the being of another. The determinant is called the cause and the determinatum is called the effect. The determinant may be synchronous with the determined or may be separated by an interval. If we take the case of clay and jar, the clay is found to continue and synchronise with the jar. But the effect is seen to follow the cause in other causes, e.g. death follows beheading.[17]

Jainas hold that causality is a sequential relation between two qualities or modes (*paryāya*). For example, when we say that the clay is the cause of the jar we are merely asserting that it is the change in the clay which appears as the jar.

Causation is a type of relation. A relation is nothing but identity-cum-difference between the given terms. Mookerjee emphasizes two characteristics of the nature of relations. First, they are all internal, having no ontological status beyond the terms. Second, they are the products of a change which occurs in the terms.[18]

Jainas do not regard a relation between terms as something which links them from outside. "In point of fact it is the terms themselves which come to have relation as an internal determination induced by changes of their nature."[19]

In western philosophy broadly two types of relations are recognized. First, the causal relation and second the logical relation. The free fall of an object under the gravitational force is the first case, while the relation between the length of a square to its area is another. In abstract mathematics relations are even "created". For example, a set may consist of (Mumbai, 2, Gandhi). The set created is entirely artificial but their elements have two types of relations. First, each belongs to the set. Second, each element has a peculiar relation to another member of belonging to the same set. This latter relation is actually known as the equivalence relation.

7. *Anekānta* As a Logical System

7.1 Logical Formula

A question that has haunted modern philosophers is whether *syādvāda* or *anekānta* can be treated as a logical system. We can discuss this problem with reference to the final stage of Jaina non-absolutism, viz. *saptabhaṅgī*.

It should be remembered that the word "logic" is ambiguous. In western philosophy the narrowest sense in which this word is used in pure logic or deductive logic is premised on the laws of thought mentioned earlier. There are thinkers such as Russell who do not recognize inductive logic as logic at all. A broader view of western logic is to include induction along with deduction.

In Indian philosophy the word logic appears to be more flexible and those who discuss an Indian system often include deductive and inductive logic, epistemology and even ontology in the broadest concept of logic. The reason is obviously the absence of uniform nomenclature and non-parallelism between the western systems, Indian *darśanas* and Indic heterodox philosophies such as Buddhist and Jaina philosophies. To avoid confusion we may use the term "pure logic" for deductive logic. The word "logic" can be used either for deductive and inductive logic or epistemology or ontology. The context will determine the sense in which the word is used.

It would be pertinent to recall that *saptabhaṅgī* is based on empiricism. The basic principle is that every object can be predicated in infinitely many ways. But for common people the seven-fold formula is necessary and sufficient to understand reality, i.e. *saptabhaṅgī,* a synthetic formula, obviates the necessity of stating all predicates of the object, which in fact is an impossible task. Another assumption is that each proposition conveys a partial truth and together the septet gives a complete truth. It is also assumed that a statement is prefixed by *syāt* to convey that the statement indicates a point of view. Without *syāt* a statement would be unconditional, which would lead to a plethora of interpretations.

This shows that we cannot treat *saptabhaṅgī* as a system of pure logic.

7.2 Many-valued Logic

Some scholars such as S. L. Pandey have conceived *nayavāda* and *syādvāda* as two formulations of many-valued logic.[1]

Consider *syādvāda* first. Pandey contends that since Jainas accept such propositions as "p and ~p" (Third proposition) they do not follow the law of contradiction. This gives rise to a third truth value. Further, *avaktavya* should be interpreted as "indeterminate" and thus should be equated with the third truth-value of Lukasiewicz's three-value logic. Pandey's system appears defective for various reasons.

1. It was explained earlier that Jainas' conjunction of p and ~p is not tantamount to their rejection of the law of contradiction. Each proposition is from a certain standpoint and p and ~p are viewed from different standpoints.
2. *Avaktavya* was discussed at length earlier. It is variously interpreted as "indeterminate", "indefinite", "uncertain", etc. Its literal translation is "inexpressible" or "indescribable". If we accept the meaning as "indeterminate" we would not be doing justice to Jainas'

concept of "inexpressible" which is considered equivalent to p and ~p "simultaneously". What's more, this "inexpressible" appears as the fourth proposition applicable to every predicate relating to an object and to all objects. In other words "inexpressible" appears universally as a *naya* in the fourth step whatever knowledge you are seeking. This is certainly not the implication of the third truth-value.

3. *Saptabhaṅgī* expresses epistemic and ontological facts and cannot be considered a piece of pure logic. The propositions of logic are connected by "or". The bivalent logic is p or ~p and the three-value logic is p or ~p or ip where ip is the indeterminate value of p. These alternatives cannot be conjoined since they are mutually exclusive.

In case of Pandey's assertion that *nayavāda* is amenable to three-value logical system, similar arguments hold good. Moreover, Pandey seems to equate *syādavāda* with *nayavāda*. This is not acceptable to Jainas since the latter contemplates a system of partially true statements while the former is *pramāṇa*, the complete knowledge. Gokhale rightly points out that *pramāṇa* cannot be an instance of *paramāṇāṃśa*.[2]

There is another hitch. It was pointed out earlier that the doctrine of *nayavāda* is sometimes considered a septet with *naigama*, etc. which is structurally different from *saptabhaṅgī* - *naya* formula. Gokhale contends that Kleen's three-valued system is more suitable to describe *saptabhaṅgī*. In Kleen's system the truth-value is undeterminable and not indeterminate. Quoting Nicholas Rescher, he asserts :

In Kleene's system a proposition is to bear the third truth-value I not for fact-related ontological reasons, but for knowledge related epistemological ones, it is not to be excluded that the proposition may in fact be true or false, is merely unknown or undeterminable what its specific truth may be.[3]

According to Gokhale, *avaktavya* should be treated as the epistemic middle. Gokhale's argument is valid in a specific case. When we know that p or ~p occurs but we are not sure which outcome has actually occurred, we invent a third category say, ip and create a triad of mutually exclusive propositions p, ~p, ip where p now means "p is proved to be true", ~p means ".not-p is proved to be true" and ip means "given the state of technology we cannot prove either p or ~p". Hence the alternative ip appears for lack of knowledge, but there is an assumption that either p or not - p should occur.

Unfortunately, *saptabhaṅgī* does not contemplate a special case where we cannot assert either p or ~p.

It is believed to be valid in all cases and in fact for all possible predicates. It is valid even in such a case as "the jar is red" where the jar is right in front of you. In such a case *avaktavya* can only mean the confusion created in the mind when two standpoints "the jar is red" and the "jar is not red" are considered "simultaneously". This confusion arises at psychological level though epistemically and ontologically the jar before you is determinate.

7.3 Modal Logic

An attempt has been made to present *saptabhaṅgī* using modal operators M (possibility) and L (necessity). *Syāt* makes a proposition conditional or from a certain standpoint, but each *syāt* appearing in the septet is a different standpoint.

Syādvāda saptabhaṅgī would appear as :

1. Mp ("perhaps p", "possibly p", etc.)
2. M~p
3. Mp.M~p
4. Mip
5. Mp.Mip
6. M~p.Mip
7. Mp.M~p.Mip

Here ip means "It is indeterminable whether p".

The above method was first suggested by S.S. Barlingay in his "*A Modern Introduction to Indian Logic*".[4]

The above representation is subject to the same criticism that was made in respect of earlier versions.

The above schemata is sometimes related to the concept of *nayas*. S. L. Pandey, for instance, thinks that *nayas* being partial knowledge can be assigned the third value I. Now, according Rescher, "With a view to the future contingency interpretation of the third-value I, Lukasiewicz introduced a modal operator of possibility and necessity (symbolically $\Diamond$ and $\Box$) into his three-valued logic."[5]. The truth table in his model appears (replacing original symbols by M and L) as follows:

p	Mp	Lp
T	T	T
I	T	F
F	F	F

If p is indeterminate ~p and ip should also be indeterminate. Hence if p stands for a *naya* then Mp, M~p, Mp.M~p, Mip, are all true. But observe that Lp is false. This is nothing but *ekāntavāda*, viz. partial truth is the whole truth. However, Jainas regard it a fallacy of *naya* (*durnaya*).

Gokhale asserts that *naya* is partial truth. Truth or falsehood of *naya* does not imply any uncertainty. *Naya*, therefore, should not be interpreted as "indeterminateness". The interpretation of *syāt* as "perhaps" is also wrong. Its better translation is "in a certain way"

7.4 Conditional Statements

Some scholars such as Sagarmal Jain and B. K. Matilal have tried to treat a *saptabhaṅgī* statement as a conditional proposition of the form "if ...then". Unfortunately this form is not suitable for *saptabhaṅgī*. The first two statements would appear as

> If x is a standpoint, the jar exists
> If y is a standpoint, the jar does not exist.

The peculiarity of the *saptabhaṅgī* statement is that a standpoint in each statement is assumed to exist but is not specified. Further, A conditional statement is a hypothetical proposition of the form :

> if p then q

It is possible that p is false but q is true. Hence the *syat* statements cannot be presented as conditional propositions.

7.5 Model of Existential Quantifier

Gokhale presents a model based on existential quantifier ∃. Let us take the first statement of *saptabhaṅgī* :

> There is a standpoint (*syāt*) that the table exists.
>
> We can write it symbolically as :[6]
>
> (∃ x) (Sx . xTp)

where xTp ≡ "x makes the proposition p true". The statement means there exists a standpoint x such that x makes p true where p ≡ the table exists.

Sx is the propositional function "x is a standpoint "

The *saptabhaṅgī* would appear as :

1. $(s\exists x)(Sx \,.\, xTp)$
2. $(\exists x)(Sx \,.\, xT{\sim}p)$
3. $(\exists x)(Sx \,.\, xTp) \,.\, (\exists y)(Sy \,.\, yT{\sim}p)$
4. $(\exists x)(Sx \,.\, xTip)$
5. $(\exists x)(Sx \,.\, xTp) \,.\, (\exists y)(Sy \,.\, yTip)$
6. $(\exists x)(Sx \,.\, xT{\sim}p) \,.\, (\exists y)(Sy \,.\, yTip)$
7. $(\exists x)(Sx \,.\, xTp) \,.\, (\exists y)(Sy \,.\, yT{\sim}p) \,.\, (\exists z)(Sz \,.\, zTip)$

You have to remember when there are more *syāts* than one in the same statement, they imply different standpoints, hence the use of different letters x, y, z. Strictly speaking, all x's and all y's are different. For example x appearing in (1) is not the same x appearing in (2) because the respective standpoints are different.

According to Gokhale this method suffers from a drawback , viz. they are statements about statements and hence have a metalinguistic character while the *syādvāda* statements are of object-linguistic character. Gokhale has tried to construct the first *bhaṅga* for "There is a standpoint such that Self is permanent". He converts the statement into "There is standpoint from which Self is permanent". Writing it as :

$\exists x\,(Sx \,.\, Fxsp)$ where S stands for Self and p for "permanent". Fxsp ≡ S is p from x which is a three-term relation.

He has not pursued the subject further because of some difficulties. For example, what is there in a standpoint on account of which we can say that one and the same statement could be true from one standpoint and false from another? He attributes this split to the fact that a sentence differs from the logician's statement. A statement is the cognitive content of an indicative sentence. It is the sense of an indicative sentence. The same sentence can be used for making different statements, some true, some false".[7] According to him, "a standpoint in this sense is an interpretation of a given sentence at least something that goes into the interpretation of a given sentence"[8].

7.6 Relational Calculus

I think it is possible to express *saptabhaṅgī* with the help of relational calculus. I will use f(x, y) to denote a relation which is usually symbolized by xRy. A triadic relation will appear as f(x, y, z). I call it relatioanal function because x, y and z are treated as variables. Moreover the order x, y, z is important. In general f(x, y, z) need not be identical with f(y, x, z).

Let f(x, y, z) mean " there exists a standpoint (x) according to which the jar (y) has existence (z)". Then *saptabhaṅgī* will appear as :

1. f(x, y, z)
2. f(x, y, ~z)
3. f(x, y, z) . f(x, y, ~z)
4. f(x, y, iz)
5. f(x, y, z) . f(x, y, iz)
6. f(x, y, ~z) . f(x, y, iz)
7. f((x, y, z) . f(x, y, ~z) . f(x, y, iz) with the identity,

$f(x, y, z) * f(x, y, \sim z) \equiv f(x, y, iz)$ where * implies simultaneity of reference.

These statements are subject to the provisos :

1. The statements pertain to a given y (subject) and a given z (predicate)
2. All x's should have different values not only in the same statement but also different statements. For example, the standpoint in statement (1) is different from the standpoint in (2).

7.7 Limitations of Symbolic Representation

It is necessary to remember that symbolic logic is based on western deductive logic, Jaina *syādvāda* is based on empiricism and includes epistemic and ontological statements which cannot be accommodated in the limited repertoire of symbols. For example, there are no separate symbols for "succession" and "simultaneity". In the last method certain provisos had to be added to the main body of the statements and I sincerely believe that I was not able to present an impeccable model consistent with Jaina thought and also western rules of mathematical logic, (e.g. "standpoint" was treated on par with the subject and predicate). The model appears to be hybrid. Even in Gokhale's model there is no symbolic distinction between standpoints in, say the first statement and the second or the fourth statement.

It seems where a system of statements involves epistemology and ontology in addition to "the laws of the mind", symbolic logic is unwieldy because a plethora of symbols will have to be used since Jaina method of investigation involves not only the mind but other faculties used in everyday life. We do not need a symbolic system because it cannot bestow any special advantage such as brevity, nor can it provide motivation or tools for further research.

8. Pre-relativity Physics

8.1 Space and Time

We cannot perceive space directly. We assume its existence, because we observe that a material body can be removed and another object can be installed in its place. We may say that space is that which can be occupied by a material body.

Aristotle believed in absolute space. He also thought that the natural state of a body was to be at rest. The body moved only if it was acted upon by a force or impulse. Moreover, like many philosophers he thought that all the laws which govern the universe can be derived by pure thought.

In physics there is a concept of rigid body. It was Poincaré who pointed out that the easiest changes we observe in the rigid body is the positional change by voluntary motion of the body. The most important change is its reversibility. The pre-relativity physics assumed that laws of a rigid body followed Euclidean geometry.

We are all familiar with Cartesian coordinates which are used to ascertain the position of a point in space.

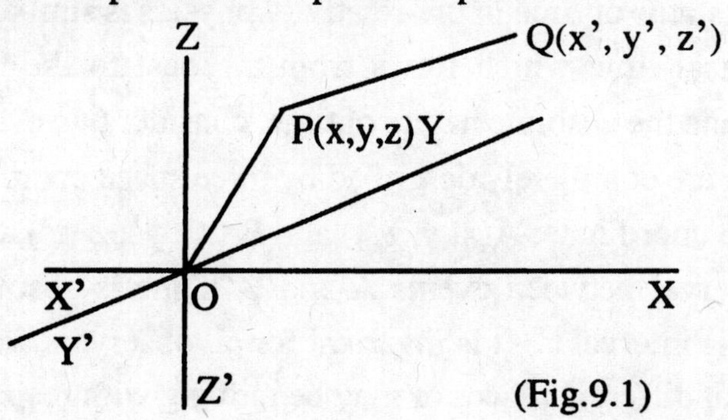

(Fig.9.1)

Fig. 9.1 shows three mutually perpendicular axes, OX, OY, OZ. If P is a point whose coordinates are x, y, z its distance from the origin O is given by

$$OP^2 = x^2 + y^2 + z^2$$

If Q is another point with coordinates (x', y', z') then the distance PQ is given by

$$PQ^2 = (x - x')^2 + (y - y')^2 + (z - z')^2$$

The characteristic of the Euclidean space is that PQ is the same for all coordinate systems. You may have a system which is moving with respect to the above system, the length PQ observed from such a system will not change. Of course, the coordinates x, y, z or x', y', z' might change and the distance of P or Q from the new origin might be different, but the interval PQ will be invariant. This appears obvious even to the lay person; if you have a rigid rod of length l you will assume that the length measured from different locations will be l. It will also remain l however the observer moves.

From the pre-relativistic angle each point is fixed in the "absolute space", but its distance from the observer changes as the latter's location alters.

The status of time in pre-relativity physics is similar. There is a universal time which flows from the past to the future. To understand the absolute nature of time, consider two events A and B which are completely described by three space coordinates and one time coordinate; A(x, y, z, t) and B (x', y', z' t'), t' - t is the time interval between events A and B. Time is absolute in the sense this interval t' - t is invariant for all observers who may be located at different places or may be moving with respect to each other. It must be remembered different observers may have different t and t' depending upon the local time they are using; what is constant is t' - t. As a corollary, if A occurs before B for a certain observer, the same order will be observed by any other observer.

It should also be remembered that space and time measurements are objective. For instance, a circle may appear elliptical to an observer who views the circle from a certain position. Such subjectivity is not admissible. It is assumed that the observer has accurate instruments to make objective recordings.

Incidentally, this is a scientific method of observation. Fortunately, Jaina philosophy, too, relies on objectivity, though it may not use sophisticated instruments for measurement to determine "standpoints" mentioned earlier.

Euclidean geometry is actually valid for the space in which we live. It is also applicable to a flat surface of two dimensions. Using the metaphor from the two dimensional geometry, the space in three dimensions is called Euclidean or flat even in Einstein's theory when the effects of gravitation are ignored.

Mathematicians have constructed different geometries theoretically; some of them have applications in the real world, while some others do not. An example of a spherical surface will elucidate how Euclidean geometry need not be useful everywhere. In Euclidean geometry, a triangle drawn on a flat surface has the well-known property; the sum of the angles of a triangle is always 180^0. This does not hold good in case of a triangle drawn on a spherical surface. In fact depending on its location, the sum of its angles may be less than or equal to or more than 180^0.

8.2 Galilean Relativity

Newton is perhaps the most famous physicist who influenced pre-relativity science. However, much of his work was made possible due to contribution by other physicists and mathematicians especially Descartes, Copernicus, Galileo and Kepler.

Nicolaus Copernicus (1473 -1548) propounded that the sun was at rest and the spinning earth moved in an orbit around the sun. Interestingly the ancient Greek astronomer Aristarchs (c 310 — 230 BCE) had proposed a similar theory much earlier. Kepler studied planetary motions and asserted that the planets moved in ellitical orbits around the sun which is at the focus of the orbits. He also propounded two other laws relating to planetary motions.

Galileo Galilei (1564-1642) an eminent physicist made immense contributions to physics. He was the first to suggest that a force applied to a body results in an acceleration and not velocity. If there is no force, a body continues to be in its state of rest or uniform motion. This is, of course, the Newton's first law of motion.

Galileo in fact had a great insight into this law. He realized that there is no absolute state of rest. Of the various bodies which are moving with uniform velocity with resect to one another, we cannot say that any particular body is at rest and the other is moving.

He makes a remarkably accurate description of the phenomena that can be observed in a ship. Suppose you are in the cabin of a large ship which is at rest with respect to the sea. You bring some butterflies and other small flying creatures. You also have a small aquarium with some fish in it. You keep a bottle filled with water inverted so that it empties drop by drop into a vessel. You will observe the butterflies and other creatures flying about, the fish moving about in the box and water falling from the bottle drop by drop.

Now suppose the ship starts moving and attains a constant velocity. When it is in a steady state without jerks, observe that all the creatures fly about as they did before. All the fish in the box move about with as much ease as they did when the ship was at rest. The drops from the inverted bottle continue to fall as before. Clearly the motion of the ship has not affected these phenomena. Galileo especially points out :

Finally the butterflies and flies continue their flights indifferently, toward every side, nor will it ever happen that they are concentrated toward the stern, as if tired out from keeping up with the course of the ship, from which they will have been separated during long intervals by keeping themselves in the air.[1]

Galilean relativity means that the concept of a frame of reference completely at rest in the universe is meaningless. Our idea of a fixed point in space is useless since the putative point cannot be tagged as a permanent fixture.

Galileo's relativity was able to answer a question that stemmed from the heliocentric theory; if the earth was moving around the sun with as high a speed as 100,000 kilometers an hour how is it that we are not aware of such a fantastic speed? The reason is that the earth's speed is irrelevant (as the ship's speed was irrelevant to the flying creatures and the fish in Galileo's description)

8.3 Relative Velocity

Of various platforms moving with respect to each other we cannot pinpoint a particular plane as "at rest", but we can speak of the velocity of a system, say S' with respect to another system S. This is the relative velocity of S' with resect to S.

If you are standing on a platform and a train passes by with a speed of 100 km/hr, you can say that it has a relative speed of 100 km/hr with respect to the platform. If another train passes by with the speed of 120 km/hr, you can easily guess that the speed of the second train with respect to the first train is 120 - 100 = 20 km/hr. This is the relative speed of the second train with respect to an observer in the first train if both trains are moving in the same direction. If the second train is moving in the opposite direction, the relative speed will be 120 + 100 = 220 km/hr.

Actually velocity having a direction and magnitude is represented by a vector $\mathbf{u} = \overrightarrow{AB}$ whose length shows the magnitude and its direction is the direction of the velocity (Fig. 9.2).

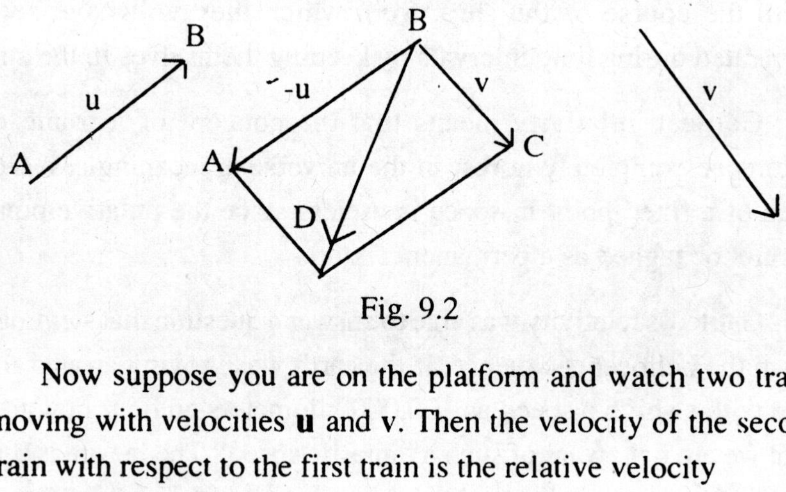

Fig. 9.2

Now suppose you are on the platform and watch two trains moving with velocities **u** and v. Then the velocity of the second train with respect to the first train is the relative velocity

v - **u** or v + (- **u**)

where -**u** = BA is a vector opposite to **u** and has the same magnitude. The addition of two vectors v and - **u** is given by the parallelogram law (v = BC). The diagonal BD of the the parallelogram ABCD is the velocity of the second train with respect to the first train.

Newtonian Physics

Newton is regarded as the greatest pre-relativity physicist not only because of his laws of motion but also because he developed complex mathematical tools used in physics. He is regarded as the inventor of differential calculus while Leibnitz is considered the author of integral calculus.

We have already mentioned Newton's first law. The second law is based on Galileo's insight. When a force acts on a body it produces an acceleration according to the formula :

Force = mass × acceleration

Acceleration is the rate of change of velocity. It is assumed in the above formula that the mass of the body does not change. If it does, then the correct formula is :

Force = rate of change of momentum

where momentum = mass × velocity

Force, acceleration and momentum are vectors and are subject to the law of vector addition or the law of parallelogram.

Newton's third law states that the force the body A exerts on body B is equal and opposite to the force B exerts on A. These forces are along the line joining A and B. (Fig. 9.3)

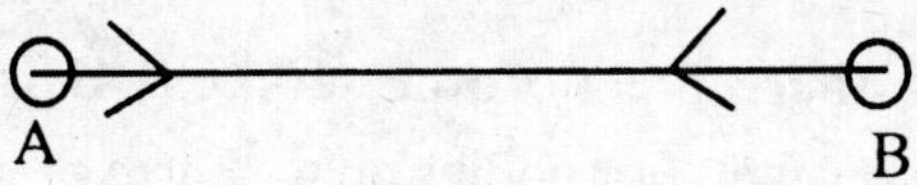

Fig. 9.3

Galileo's experiments with falling bodies under gravitation are well known. He found that the time taken by two bodies released from the same height to reach the ground is independent of their masses. This result is accurate when the air resistance is ignored.

He also found that when a body slides down a smooth inclined plane, the velocity it acquires when it reaches the ground is just sufficient to allow it to reach the original height. His observations lead to what is called the law of conservation of energy. When the body at rest is at a height it has a potential energy stored into it. When it reaches the ground the whole of the potential energy is converted into kinetic energy. This kinetic energy is sufficient to lift it to its original height.

When Galilean relativity is combined with this conservation law, one is led to other conservation laws, viz. conservation of momentum, conservation of angular momentum. (The angular momentum of a body revolving about an axis is the product of its momentum and its perpendicular distance from the axis) and the conservation of the mass of a body. While many scientists contributed to Newtonion physics it was Newton himself who integrated different discoveries and expressed them in the form of elegant mathematics.

8.4 Inverse Square Laws

According to the laws of gravitation if m and m' are two masses and r is the distance between them, the force of attraction between them is given by

$$F = G\,(mm'/r^2)$$

assuming there are no other forces. G is known as the gravitational constant. For bodies on the earth or close to the earth, if m' is the mass of the earth, r the distance between any mass m and the earths'centre. This distance may be taken as constant approximately equal to the radius of the earth, provided m is not at a great height. Gm'/r^2 is thus a constant (g) and we get

$$F = mg$$

This is how we write F the gravitational force on mass m; g is the gravitational acceleration which doesn not depend on m.

There are also other inverse square laws; electric and magnetic forces act in a similar way. If q, q' are electric charges in vacuum the force between them is

$$F = qq'/r^2$$

If m, m' are magnetic pole strenghts, the force between them is

$$F = mm'/r^2$$

However, electric and magnetic forces are repulsive as well as attractive. Like poles repel while unlike poles attract. It should be remembered that magnetic poles cannot be isolated in practice, but the equation for the magnetic force given above is for hypothetically isolated poles.

There is some difficulty in understanding how these various forces act. For example, in case of two heavenly bodies separated by thousands of miles how does the gravitational force between them arise? It was thought that this force acted almost instantaneously. This concept remained a puzzle for a long time under the name "action at a distance."

8.5 Fields

Newtonian dynamics worked very well in most cases. Even in case of light his assumption that it consists of tiny particles appeared to explain some optical properties. However, Newton's ideas seemed to be inadequate when physicists encountered interference of light where two beams of light could give rise to bright and dark bands. How could light particles hitting each other lead to mutual cancellation? It was then proposed that light was a wave motion. It was postulated that these waves traveled in a medium called "ether". Under this hypothesis, ether consisted of material particles, though scientists could not detect the putative ether.

Physicists soon found that magnetism and electricity were closely related. A moving electric charge gave rise to a magnetic field. A swift movement of a magnet through a coil created an electric current in the coil. While some of these phenomena could be accommodated in Newton's scheme of things, physicists found it increasingly difficult to explain electromagnetic phenomena with mathematical elegance.

The concept of a field soon became ascendent especially when particle mechanics of Newton appeared to fail. The physicist who made a magnificent contribution to the field theory was Michael Farady (1791 — 1867)

Most of us have performed the experiment at school in which iron filings are placed on the paper below which lies a bar magnet. The filings appear to form curved lines emanating from the magnet especially from the ends. We call them the magnetic lines of force. The concept of a field is not dependent on the iron filings. Even when the filings are absent the field is assumed to exist physically coinciding with the lines of force mentioned above. In fact the concept can be further refined. It indicates at every point outside the magnet a vector along which an imagined isolated north pole would travel. The field is also quantified; its magnitude is the force experienced by the imagined north pole of unit strength. (The north pole of a magnet approximately indicates earth's geographical North, when suspended freely.)

The concept of a the electric field is similar. The field at a point (near an electric charge or current) is represented by a vector whose direction indicates how a positive charge will move when it is placed at that point. Its magnitude is the force experienced by a unit positive charge.

A gravitational field is similarly visualized. All these fields are vector fields.

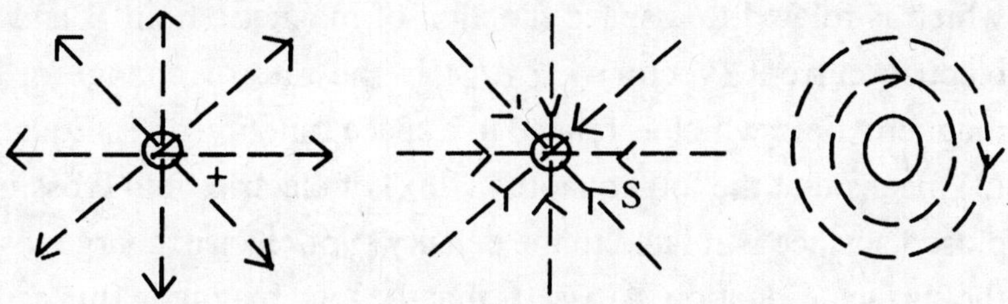

(a) (b) (c)

Fig. 9.3 Electric and magnetic fields

(a) Positive electric charge, (b) South magnetic pole, (c) Magnetic field due to an electric current going into the paper.

8.6 Electromagnetic Waves

Faraday's extensive experiments with magnets and coils convinced him that electric and magnetic fields were real or "physical stuff". He guessed that electric and magnetic fields could travel in empty space like waves. He even suggested that light could be a manifestation of such waves.

Several scientists such as Gauss, Faraday, Ampere (1775 — 1836) have contributed to electricity and magnetism and their interaction with one another greatly increased the knowledge of electromagnetism.

It was, however, James Clerk Maxwell (1831 — 1879) who integrated various results and came out with his famous equations:

(1) $1/c^2\ \partial \mathbf{E}/\partial t = \text{curl } \mathbf{B} - 4\pi \mathbf{j}$

(2) $\partial \mathbf{B}/\partial t = -\text{curl}\ \mathbf{E}$

(3) $\text{div}\ \mathbf{E} = 4\pi\rho$

(4) $\text{div}\ \mathbf{B} = 0$

In these equations $\partial \mathbf{E}/\partial t$ is the rate of change of electric field which is related to a space function of magnetic field **B** and the electric current (vector) **j**. $\partial \mathbf{B}/\partial t$ is the rate of change of the magnetic field which is related to a space function of **E**. Equation (3) means that the total quantity (flux) of electric field crossing a closed surface is related to the density ρ of electric charge inside the surface. Equation (4) asserts that the total magnetic flux across such a closed surface is zero because unlike electric charges magnetic poles cannot be isolated.

These equations imply that magnetic and electric fields "push" each other. They actually combine Faraday's experimental results and Maxwell's theoretical conjectures; an oscillating magnetic field would give rise to an oscillating electric field which in turn would cause an oscillating magnetic field and so on. What is most astonishing is that "c" which appears in the equations is the velocity with which these two fields propagate in vacuum and equals exactly the velocity of light.

This propagating complex field thus identified with light whose velocity is about 186,000 miles per second. Moreover, this theory could explain the interference and polarization phenomena of light.

In plane polarization electric oscillations are in one plane ("plane of polarization") perpendicular to the propagation of light and the magnetic field oscillates in another plane which is perpendicular to the plane of polarization as well as the direction of the propagation of light. (Fig. 9.4)

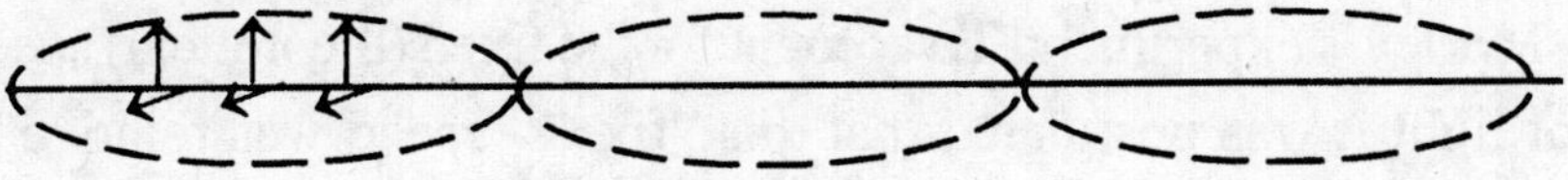

Fig. 9.4

It was conjectured that visible light is only a small range of wavelengths (4 -7 10^{-7}m) and the larger portion of electromagnetic waves consisted of radiation that is not visible. Heinrich Hertz in 1880 was able to produce electromagnetic waves artificially by passing currents through conductors.

Maxwell's theory tells us that light need not be considered as a flow of particles. It can be treated as a range of electromagnetic waves which travel with a speed of c.

Maxwell was able to calculate the quantum of energy which was carried by the electromagnetic waves.

In the four equations mentioned above, if we put $\rho = 0$ and $\mathbf{j} = 0$ we have the case of empty space. The equations lead to what is called the wave equation or D'Alembert equation which is a simple form of Maxwell's equations.

8.7 Michelson and Morley

An experiment of great importance was performed by Michelson and Morley in 1887. Recall how an observer from one moving train measures the relative velocity of another moving train. Now, the earth moves around the sun at the speed of 100,000 miles per hour. If we measure the speed of light in the direction of earth's motion (when it is moving towards the source of light), it would be more than the speed we record when the light is at right angles to the earth's motion. To their surprise, the physicists found that the speed of light was constant. Of course, Maxwell's prediction (1868) of the constancy of the velocity of light preceded Michelson

- Morley's experiment. To account for the fixed (theoretical) speed of light it was postulated that this "fixed" speed was relative to the all-pervading medium "ether". But to the observers who were moving with different velocities relative to the ether the velocity of light would be different depending upon their respective velocities. This created a new riddle.

We will see in the next chapter how the conundrum of the velocity of light was ultimately solved by Einstein.

9. The Theory of Special Relativity

9.1 Dilemma

We now face a dilemma. Our experience tells us that Galilean relativity is valid; of various frames of reference moving with uniform velocity relative to one another, no system can be treated as fixed or at rest. But Galilean theory would require that the velocity observed from these moving frames would be different depending on their relative velocities. For example, an observer who is moving against light would find the velocity of light greater than the observer who is moving with light rays. But Maxwell's theory and Michelson-Morley's experiment mentioned in chapter 8 proves that the velocity of light is a universal constant, c.

Lorentz tried to explain Michelson-Morley's results under the assumption that the forces that bind matter together are electromagnetic in nature. Hence the material bodies should obey Maxwell's equations. One of the theoretical predictions Lorentz made was that a body which moved with a velocity close to the velocity of light would appear to shrink in the direction of motion. This effect is called FitzGerald-Lorentz contraction. However, although his prediction of contraction proved to be correct. Lorentz had used logic based on physical forces and his theory could not last long.

We must mention Poincaré, a great mathematician who seems to have almost solved the conundrum. As Penrose points out:

> Poincaré, outstanding mathematician that he was, was able to show (in 1905) that there is an exact way for matter to

> behave, according to the relativity principle underlying Maxwell's equations, so that uniform motion cannot be detected at all. He also obtained much understanding of the physical implications of this principle (including the "relativity of simultaneity"...). He appears to have regarded it as just *one* possibility, and did not share Einstein"s conviction that some relativity principle "must" hold.[1]

Einstein insisted that a relativity principle based on constancy of the velocity of light did hold good. The result was that Galilean relativity had to be modified, not abandoned.

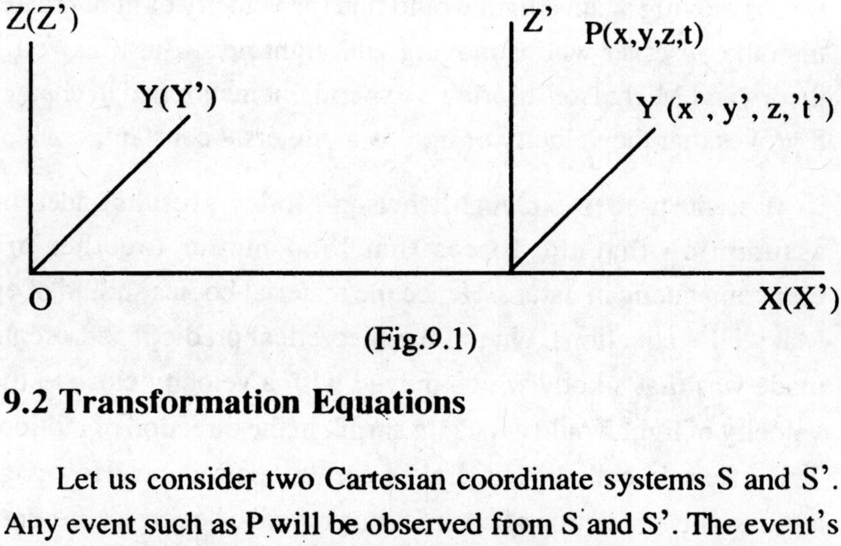

(Fig.9.1)

9.2 Transformation Equations

Let us consider two Cartesian coordinate systems S and S'. Any event such as P will be observed from S and S'. The event's coordinates observed from S and S' will be represented by (x, y, z, t) and (x', y', z', t'). Suppose initially S and S' coincide. At t = t' = 0, S' begins to move along x axes (OX and OX') with a uniform velocity v with respect to S. (Fig. 9.1). A little introspection will convince you that after time t, S and S' should be related as follows:

$$x' = x - vt$$

$y' = y$

$z' = z$

$t' = t$ ...(1)

These are the equations in pre-relativity physics and are called the transformation equations. Time being absolute, $t = t'$. Moreover it is assumed that there are no changes along y and z directions which are perpendicular to the direction of motion.

However, when we assume that the velocity of light is constant, we are dealing with Einstein's special relativity. These equations are difficult to derive and we will only write them down.

$x' = (x - vt) / (\sqrt{1 - (v^2/c^2)})$

$y' = y$

$z' = x$

$t' = (t - (v/c^2)x) / (\sqrt{1 - (v^2/c^2)})$ ...(2)

It should be obvious to you that both x' and t' are modified and involve c.

When v is quite small compared with c, $v/c = 0$ and equations (2) reduce to (1), and Einstein's relativity agrees with pre-relativity transformation equations. This suggests that for small velocities we can ignore relativistic effects and use pre-relativity physics. This also shows that what we called Galilean relativity is approximately valid and special relativity is only a modification. Equations (2) are called Lorentz transformation equations.

We must realize that special relativity obviates the necessity of the existence of the medium called ether.

From equations (2) we can get (x, y, z, t) in terms of (x', y', z', t')

$$x = (x' + vt') / (\sqrt{1 - (v^2/c^2)})$$

$$y = y'$$

$$z = z'$$

$$t = (t' + (v/c^2)x') / (\sqrt{1 - (v^2/c^2)}) \qquad ...(3)$$

This shows that S has a relative velocity (-v) with respect to S'.

9.3 Moving Clock

Suppose we attach firmly a clock to S' at x_0', then t in (3) can be written as

$$t = ((v/c^2)x_0' + t') / (\sqrt{1 - (v^2/c^2)}) \qquad ...(4)$$

From this we can compare an S - time interval $t_2 - t_1$ with the corresponding interval $t_2' - t_1'$

$$t_2 - t_1 = (t_2' - t_1')/ (\sqrt{1 - (v^2/c^2)})$$

From the viewpoint of S, the clock appears to slow down. But something more can be inferred from equation (4). The further (x_0') is the clock from the origin O', the slower it appears to go.

We can derive similar equations for t' in terms of t. We shall arrive at similar conclusion : An S-clock fixed at, say the origin O, appears to go slow for an observer in S'. Moreover, the further the clock is on the left (negative) side of O, the slower it appears. This phenomenon is usually captured in ordinary parlance as "moving clocks go slow".

9.4 Lorentz Contraction

A moving rigid rod shows a similar relativistic effect. Suppose a rigid rod is fixed on S' along x' axis (which coincides with x axis of S). If its length measured in S' is l' and its length as observed from S is l then it can be proved that

$$l = (\sqrt{1 - (v^2/c^2)})\, l'$$

Thus the rod appears to have shrunk by the factor $(\sqrt{1 - (v^2/c^2)})$. Similarly a rod fixed in S along x axis will appear to contract when observed from S'

This phenomenon is called FitzGerald-Lorentz contraction.

Peter Bergmann has summarized these two results succinctly : [2]

Every clock appears to go at its fastest rate when it is at rest relatively to the observer. If it moves relatively to the observer with velocity v, its rate appears slowed down by the factor $(\sqrt{1 - (v^2/c^2)})$. Every rigid body appears to be longest when at rest relatively to the observer. When it is not at rest, it appears contracted in the direction of its relative motion by the factor $(\sqrt{1 - (v^2/c^2)})$ while the direction perpendicular to the direction of motion is unaffected

9.5 Minkowski's Space-time

In classical physics, the distance PQ between point P and Q is invariant for all systems of coordinates. In special relativity we can prove that there exists a space-time interval which is invariant with respect to systems which move with relative uniform velocities with respect to one another. That interval Δs is given by

$$\Delta s^2 = (x_2 - x_1)^2 + (y_2 - y_1)^2 + (z_2 - z_1)^2 - c^2(t_2 - t_1)^2 \qquad ...5$$

where (x_1, y_1, z_1, t_1) and (x_2, y_2, z_2, t_2) are two events observed from a system. We can write this briefly as

$$\Delta s^2 = \Delta x^2 + \Delta y^2 + \Delta z^2 - c^2 \Delta t^2 \qquad ...6$$

If we write ict = w (where $i = \sqrt{-1}$) this becomes

$$\Delta s^2 = \Delta x^2 + \Delta y^2 + \Delta z^2 + \Delta w^2 \qquad ...7$$

Δs is precisely the space-time interval which is invariant in spacial relativity. Note that this resembles the interval (length) in pre-relativity physics with one more "dimension" w added. Sometimes the negative of Δs^2 in (6) is taken as the measure of the space-time interval. Thus

$$\Delta s^2 = - \Delta x^2 - \Delta y^2 - \Delta z^2 + c^2 \Delta t^2 \qquad ...8$$

Minkowski (1864 - 1909) who was Einstein's teacher looked upon this world in which space and time are entangled as the four-dimensional world. In his famous lecture at the university of Göttingen in 1908, he declared :

> Henceforth space by itself, and time by itself, are doomed to fade away into mere shadows, and only a kind of union of the two will preserve an independent reality.[3]

The space-time interval mentioned above pertains to the Euclidean space-time in four dimensions x, y, z, t.

9.6 Light Cone

We can have a greater insight into the four dimensional world if we plot a graph of time (t axis) against space. Since we cannot have a four dimensional diagram, we will show only two spatial axes, i.e. one axis (y) is suppressed without causing the loss of generality. To simplify matters, let us suppose an explosion takes place at t = 0 at the origin O. Then the light emitted will travel at velocity c with equation

$$x^2 + y^2 + z^2 - c^2t^2 = 0 \qquad \ldots 9$$

(Fig.9.1)

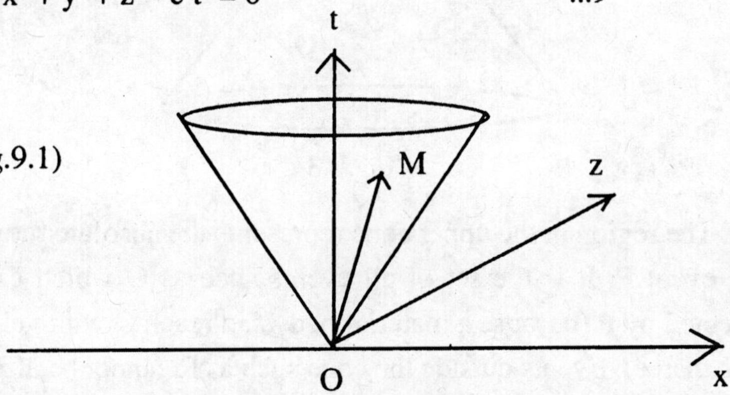

The graph of t against space appears as a cone with the apex at O. The cone divides space-time into three regions. The first region is the surface of the cone along which the light travels according to equation (9). Note that for light trajectory the interval $\Delta s = 0$. The second region is the inside of the cone. If a material particle starts moving from O at t = 0, its graph (OM) will be in the interior, because its velocity is less than c. The third region is outside the cone. No signal can pass from O in this region because the region indicates a velocity greater than c, which is impossible.

Now we can take any point P in space not necessarily O. Actually P has four coordinates x, y, z, t and hence it represents an event. The upper cone is called the future light cone of this event. We can similarly draw a cone below P which is the past cone of P.

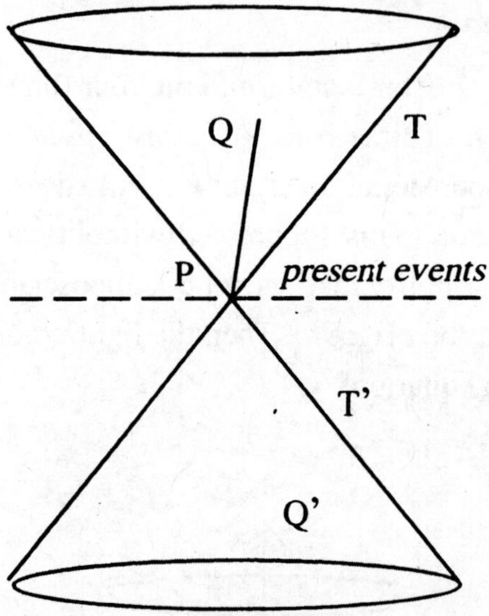

Fig.9.3

The region in the upper cone represents the absolute future of the event P. It is the set of all events such as Q which can be affected by P (because a material body can reach Q with velocity less than c). Events outside the cone such as R cannot be affected by P because PR can be traversed only by a velocity greater than c, which is impossible. Any event T on the surface is nothing but the light signal from P which can just reach T. Similarly, the absolute past of P is an event inside the lower cone. Any event such as Q' can affect P. No event outside the cone such as R' can affect P and any event such as T' can just be connected with P by a light signal along the surface.[4]

Before we proceed, two comments are necessary. If you refer to transformation equation (3) you will find an expression ($\sqrt{1 - (v^2/c^2)}$) in the denominator. This becomes zero when $v = c$, and imaginary when v is greater than c. The conclusion is that no signal can travel faster than light for which $v = c$ and a material body can travel only with a velocity less than c. Second, two events which appear simultaneously from one system need not be simultaneous when viewed from another system.

9.7 Addition of Velocities

Suppose we have three frames of reference S, S', S". S' has the velocity v with respect to S and S" has the velocity w with respect to S'. Then what is the relative velocity of S" with respect to S? It should be obivious to you that this velocity u is just the addition of v and w as we learnt in school physics. Thus u = v + w assuming for simplicity that v and w are in the same direction. But using Lorentz transformations successively, it can be proved that in relativity u is modified :

$$u = (v + w) / (1 + vw/c^2)$$

when v and w are small compared with c, vw/c^2 is is negligible and we get back u = v + w.

9.8 Mass and Energy

It can be proved using special relativity equations that energy can be converted into mass and vice versa under suitable conditions. Hence the law of conservation of mass and the conservation of energy are integrated into a conservation law of mass-energy. The famous equation relating the mass of a particle to its energy (E) is given by

$$E = mc^2$$

This law is proved beyond doubt in the behavior of elementary or subatomic particles. For example, when uranium atom decays, it splits into smaller pieces. It is found that the mass of the decaying atom is less than the total of component masses. The difference has been converted into the kinetic energy of the moving components according to $E = mc^2$.

Another example may be illustrated. In quantum theory light has a dual personality; it behaves like a wave as well as a beam of particles called photons which have zero mass. There is a subatomic particle called π^0 mason. It has a positive mass but it decays into two photons rapidly. One half of π^0 mass gets converted into each photon in the form of energy. (Remember a photon has no mass)

9.9 The Earth and the Sun

Hawking illustrates an interesting case of the sun's light cone and its effect on us.[5] Fig. 9.4 shows the light cone of the sun whose apex is some moment P.

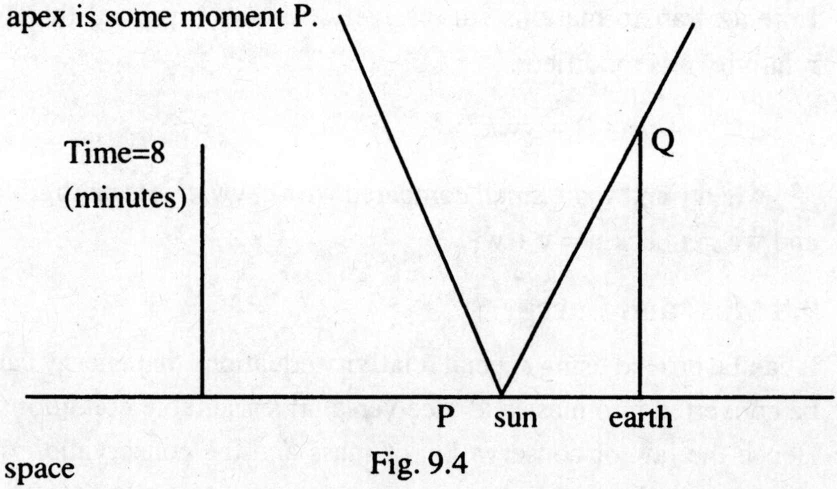

Fig. 9.4

The earth's world-line (i.e. the graph of time against space) is a vertical line. It takes the sun-light about 8 minutes to reach the earth. The earth's world-line meets the cone at Q at $t = 8$. Suppose the sun suddenly "dies" at P. Then the earth enters the future P-cone of the sun only at Q and hence the sun cannot affect the earth below Q. We would be unaware of the sun's death till we reach Q. Similarly, we may see stars millions of light years away, but we really do not know what is happening there right now. We are all only witnessing the state of these stars as they existed millions of years ago.

9.10 Poincaré Motion

Two frames of reference moving with uniform velocity with respect to each other are equivalent to each other in special relativity or Minkowskian geometry.

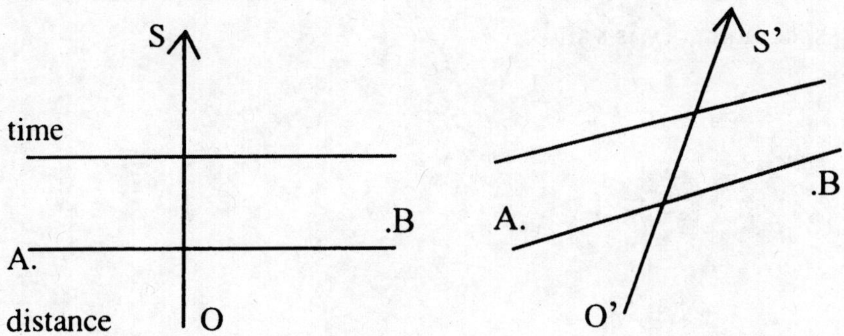

Fig. 9.5

Suppose we have two such systems having observers S ("stationary") and S' ("moving"). In fig. 9.5 space-times are shown only in two dimensions. OS shows the world line of S while the horizontal lines are planes perpendicular to the plane of the paper. Each horizontal line shows the plane at constant t. Hence each line shows the simultaneous space for S. If the relevant equations are transformed to the frame of S', you will find all "simultaneous spaces" become tilted. This transformation depicts a rigid motion in Minkowskian space-time and is called a Poincaré motion.

A and B are two events. For S, A occurs before B while for S', B occurs before A. (Compare their relative positions with respect to simultaneous spaces in each case). The reason for this reversal is that "simultaneous spaces" of S and S' are different. It is necessary to understand that events A and B are "spatially separated" i.e. each lies outside the light cone of the other. In such a case a material particle cannot travel from one event to the other.

Subatomic particles travel at a very high speed comparable with the velocity of light. Their behaviour affords an opportunity to observe that their trajectories do not conform to pre-relativistic dynamics. Relativity equations correctly describe their behaviour. Experiments with subatomic particles have proved that Einstein's special theory is valid.

10. The General Theory of Relativity

10.1 Inertial and Gravitational Masses

In chapter 9 we considered a special case, viz. inertial frames of reference, i.e. the systems which moved with uniform velocities with respect to one another. Einstein, however, was not satisfied with his derivation. Why should we consider only a special case? He rightly observes :[1]

Just as it was consistent from the Newtonian standpoint to make both the statements, *tempus est absolutum, spatium est absolutum*, so from the standpoint of the special theory of relativity we must say, *continuum spatii et temporis est absolutum.*

In this latter statement *absolutum* means not only physically real but also independent in its physical properties, having a physical effect, but not itself influenced by physical condition. He realized special theory merely shifts absoluteness of space and time to another absoluteness viz. absoluteness of the space-time continuum.

He thought that it was against the spirit of science to conceive of a thing such as space-time continuum which acts itself, but which cannot be acted upon. He also thought it odd that relativity principle should be confined to the special case of inertial frames.

He had an insight into a strange phenomenon which was earlier observed by Galileo, the time taken by different bodies dropped from the same height to reach the ground was the same, independent of their masses. Of course, the air resistance was ignored.

He reasoned that actually there are two masses, inert and gravitational. The mass which is pulled by the earth is the gravitational mass m_g which experiences a force $F = m_g g$. This force is resisted by the inertial mass m_i and the resultant acceleration is F/m_i or $m_g g/m_i$. But the Galilean experiments show that all falling bodies have the same acceleration, viz. g. Hence $m_g g/m_i = g$, from which $m_g/m_i = 1$, or $m_g = m_i$, i.e. the intert mass equals the gravitational mass. We are so much accustomed to treating these masses as equal that we do not realize that this equality is due to the particular type of force (gravitational) involved. For example, in case of two electric charges q, q' the force is given by

$$F = q\,q'/r^2 \qquad \text{(chapter 8)}$$

and the acceleration of say q will be given by $q\,q'/mr^2$; the mass m of q is not cancelled and the acceleration (unlike in the gravitational case) is dependent on m.[2]

Moreover, the equality of m_g and m_i has been proved experimentally by Eötvös with great accuracy.

10.2 Principle of Equivalence

Now consider two systems A and A'. A is an inertial system. A mass (assuming there is no other mass nearby to attract it) will have a uniform velocity with respect to A. (zero velocity is not barred). Suppose the other system A' is uniformly accelerated (with acceleration a) with respect to A. Then this mass will also be accelerated with respect to A'. In fact all such bodies (ignoring the mutual attractive forces) will have equal and parallel accelerations a, independent of their masses. Actually all these masses will behave in the same way as if a gravitational field equal to a is present in A'. Hence with respect to these masses we can treat the scenario in any one of the following ways :

(1) A is the only system which is allowable, there being no gravitational field. A' is merely an accelerating system.

(2) A' is "at rest" but has a gravitational field equal to a.

In this way, the accelerated system becomes an equivalent "stationary" system with a gravitational field. What Einstein has achieved is that using the equality of interial and gravitational masses, he has done away with special inertial systems or rather integrated them with accelerated systems which are now treated as systems with gravitation. This is called the principle of equivalence; A can now be treated on par with A' (with gravitational filed).

This acceleration-gravitation equivalence is actually felt in an elevator. When the elevator begins to ascend with acceleration, the rider feels an increase in the gravitational field. When the elevator begins to descend with acceleration, there is a feeling of decreased gravitational pressure for the rider. If the elevator cable were to break, then there would be a free fall. The rider would "float" in relation to the elevator because the acceleration is cancelled by the gravitational force, till the elevator hits the ground.

10.3 Generalized Coordinates

Special relativity is applicable to flat space-time where the "interval" Δs can be written as:

$$\Delta s^2 = -\Delta x^2 - \Delta y^2 - \Delta z^2 + c^2\Delta t^2$$

Unfortunately, this is valid only when there is absence of gravitational field. However, if we can take any infinitesimal space-time ds where two events separated by the interval ds are extremely close we can write the above equation as:

$$ds^2 = -dx^2 - dy^2 - dz^2 + c^2dt^2 \quad \dots (3)$$

Usually we do not come across a finite region where the space-time is flat. Hence we have to use a generalized or curvilinear coordinate system, where x_1, x_2, x_3, x_4 are four coordinates not necessarily those involved in (3). The geometry of such coordinates was studied by Gauss and Riemann. It is Riemannian geometry that needs to be used in general relativity. For such coordinates ds can be written as

$$ds^2 = g_{11}dx_1^{\ 2} + g_{22}dx_1^{\ 2} + ... + 2g_{12}dx_1dx_2 + 2g_{13}dx_1dx_3 + ...$$

which involve not only squares of dx_1, dx_2, etc. but also their products. This can be written as

$$ds^2 = \Sigma g_{\mu\nu} dx_\mu dx_\nu \qquad ...(4)$$

where the summation Σ for μ and ν ranges from 1 to 4. There are in all 10 terms, because there is some symmetry such as dx_{12} = dx_{21}, etc. The term $g_{\mu\nu}$ is called the metric tensor of the second rank . Thus space in which (4) appears is called a Riemannian space. In Riemannian space when we go over from one system to another, ds is invariant. Note that (3) shows a special case of flat space-time where Cartesian coordinates can be used. A simple case where Cartesian coordinates cannot be used is a spherical surface which was mentioned earlier.

Riemannian space-time is difficult to deal with and its transformation equations are extremely complicated involving tensor analysis. We cannot pursue its mathematics further.

The Riemannian space-time is called curved because it is not always possible to reduce (4) to (3), the latter being flat space-time where four dimensional Minkowskian geometry can be used. It is the presence of gravitation which makes a space-time curved. You will notice that incorporation of gravitational field into the metric "ds" shows the "geometrization" of space-time and gravity just as the four dimensional Minkowskian space-time was geometrization of time as the fourth dimension.

10.4 Geodesic

In Euclidean geometry a geodesic is the straight line joining any two points, which is the shortest distance between them. In case of a spherical surface, too, it is the shortest distance *along* the surface. In this case, the two neighboring geodesics which are initially parallel tend towards each other. This curvature is called positive. On the other hand, on a saddle-like surface you encounter a negative curvature, i.e. two neighbouring geodesics which are parallel tend to diverge.

This concept of curvature can be used in space-time. In Minkowskian world where there is no gravitational force, the space-time is flat which has zero curvature. When gravitational field exists, Minkowskian geometry is only approximate; the space-time is now curved. However, at any point it may be called "locally flat".

We mentioned the worldline of a body in chapter 9. Geodeisics are nothing but world lines in which the space-time interval ds is minimized. Sometimes the interval ds is taken as the negative of what was earlier written as ds^2 in chapter 9. In a flat space-time it would appear as :

$$ds^2 = -dx^2 - dy^2 - dz^2 + c^2dt^2$$

This form was used in equation 3 of section 10.3. In Riemannian geometry ds^2 will stand similarly modified. In such a case the space-time is maximized.

All the planets and heavenly bodies and even light follow their own geodesics. For example, light particles (photons) travel in a straight line, but they are slightly bent near a massive gravitational field such as that of the sun.

10.5 Relativism within Relativity

It is interesting to observe how geometrization of space-time leads to non-absolutism. First, in absence of a gravitational field the invariant space-time appears as :

$$ds^2 = -dx^2 - dy^2 - dz^2 + c^2dt^2$$

Since space and time are intricately entangled because time interval now becomes relative, we say that time is the fourth dimension and hence we get Minkowskian world. But is this geometry real or is it a metaphor? There are two opinions. The first is that we treat Minkowsky world as a four dimensional world as mere mathematical convenience. In reality time does not behave like space. The second opinion is that we really live in a four dimensional world and space and time should be replaced by space-time.

The reason, of course, is that in Euclidean geometry the invariant was :

$$ds^2 = dx^2 + dy^2 + dz^2 \quad ...(5)$$

But because of constancy of the speed of light we have a new invariant

$$ds^2 = -dx^2 - dy^2 - dz^2 + c^2dt^2 \quad ...(6)$$

Hence we have two relative views of the same reality either (1) time interval is relative or (2) time is the fourth dimension.

Similarly while going from special relativity to general relativity the invariant becomes

$$ds^2 = g_{11}dx^2 + g_{22}dy^2 + g_{33}dz^2 + ... \quad ...(7)$$

This again can be looked upon in two ways. We can say that there is a field of force which makes the invariant (6) change to (7). The other view would be, gravitation is a fiction. Actually it is a different geometry given by (7). But if we assume the geometry (6) or Euclidean space-time to be true, there appears a discrepancy in the form of a force on a particle which we call gravitational field. In reality we have a different type of geometry, viz. Riemannian geometry and we mistakenly assumed Euclidean geometry to exist. Frankly, of these two views we cannot conclusively say which is the "true" view.

It would be interesting to compare geodesics in flat and curved space-time (Fig. 10.1)

(a) In the flat space-time light travels in a straight line along the surface of cones which are parallel.

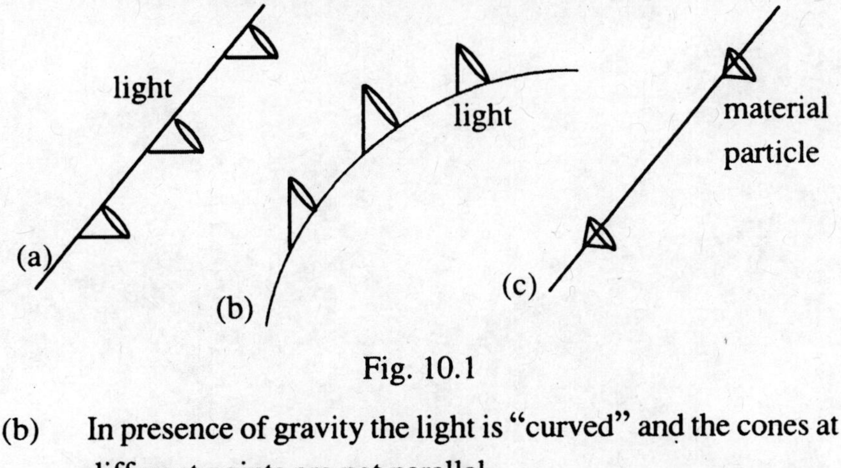

Fig. 10.1

(b) In presence of gravity the light is "curved" and the cones at different points are not parallel.

(c) Material particles always travel inside the cone.

Einstein's general relativity has already been proved. The theory predicts that a clock goes slightly slower in a gravitational field. This effect has been verified. Physicists have also gathered enough evidence to show that electromagnetic radiation is bent by the sun. There was an anomaly in the motion of the planet Mercury, known as the "prehelian advance", in Newtonian physics. Using Einstein's theory the anomaly has been eliminated.

General relativity predicts the existence of gravitational waves similar to electromagnetic waves travelling with the same speed. Observations by astronomers on what is called binary pulsar system closely agree with the hypothesis of the emission of gravitational waves, though this only indirectly supports the existence of such waves.

11. Non-absolutism in the Quantum World

11.1 Matter - Wave Duality

The quantum theory is closely associated with relativity theory and is equally revolutionary. Non-absolutism abounds in the quantum world, the strange world of light and subatomic particles.

In 1900, Max Planck discovered that electromagnetic oscillations occur only in "quanta" or packets of energy. This was surprising because as waves, electromagnetic fields should emerge or be absorbed continuously. The energy E of these discrete quanta was found to be

$$E = h\nu$$

where ν is the frequency of the radiation and h is Planck's constant, which is quite small (6.6×10^{-34} Joule seconds). This conundrum of "energy bundles" was solved by Einstein who hypothesized that electromagnetic radiation including light can exist only in discrete units. These units are now called photons. Strangely, Newton's corpuscular theory was vindicated in some sense.

In 1923, De Broglie, a French physicist pushed the particle-wave dichotomy further. He proposed that just as light behaved with dual nature of particle-wave, even matter should show this duality. Thus an electron of mass m should behave like a wave of frequency ν given by

$$h\nu = E = mc^2$$

in which Einstein's and Planck's equations are combined. This hypothesis was confirmed later. In fact this principle is used in electron microscope.

This suggests that a wave can be treated as matter and vice versa. However, these "matter waves" can be observed only at the microlevel, i.e. in case of electrons, protons, etc. We have now relativism not only in respect of mass-energy but also in respect of matter-wave.

11.2 Single Particle as Wave

A more astonishing aspect of this duality appears in an experiment known as the two-slit experiment.

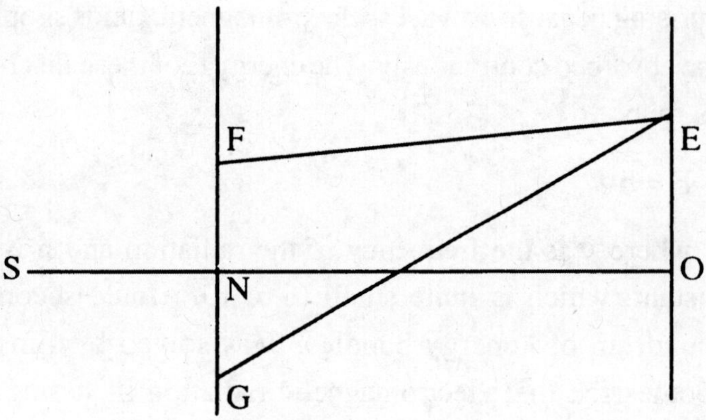

Fig. 11.1

In Fig. 11.1, S is the source which emits photons or elementary particles such as electrons. To be specific. Let S be a source of monochromatic light, i.e. it emits light of a single frequency. F, G are narrow slits FN = GN. EO is a screen perpendicular to the plane of the paper.

Suppose initially only one slit is open. The light will pass through it and spread out. When there is sufficient intensity, the illumination of the screen is fairly uniform. However, when the intensity is reduced, you find the picture "spotty" showing that light indeed consists of individual particles or photons.

Fig. 11.2

Now the second slit is opened. When the light is sufficiently strong you find an interference pattern. In this case F and G act as secondary sources of light. We have now two rays FE and GE which meet on the screen. Now both these rays are waves as shown in Fig. 11.2. When two such waves are superimposed, interference takes place.

When E is at such a distance that the crests (or troughs) of both waves fall on each other, there is reinforcement and the intensity is four times the original intensities of FE and GE. If on the hand, the trough of one falls on the crest of another, there is total cancellation and darkness appears. In the intermediate cases there is a mixed picture of varying intensities.

This phenomenon can be explained only on the basis of the wave theory. If we use the corpuscular theory, how can we explain the destructive interference or darkness? How can we conceive that one photon cancels the other?

However, what is surprising is that when the flow is reduced to one photon, interference continues. Does a photon split and the truncated portions pass through the two slits? How can the photon pass through both the slits? Physicists do not subscribe to the view that the photon breaks up. But what is demonstrated is that even a single photon can act as a wave.

We have omitted many interesting results of the experiment since they are not relevant to the central theme of matter-wave duality. It is worth mentioning what physicists think. To quote Penrose :[1]

> But here things are very different : each individual photon behaves like a wave entirely on its own! In some sense, each particle travels through both slits at once and it interferences with itself.

The dual nature of the photon may be described in terms of *saptabhaṅgī*:

1. There is a viewpoint (*syāt*) that the photon is a particle.
2. *Syāt* the photon is not a particle (because it appears to interfere with itself).
3. *Syāt* the photon is a particle and the photon is not a particle.
4. *Syāt* the photon is indescribable.
5. *Syāt* the photon is a particle and is indescribable.
6. The photon is not a particle and is indescribable.
7. The photon is a particle, not a particle and is indescribable.

11.3 Non-absolutism in Measurement

Closely associated with matter-wave duality is the well-known uncertainty principle enunciated by Heisenberg. According to this it is not possible to measure both the position and momentum of a particle accurately at the same time. If Δx, Δp show accuracies of position and momentum respectively, $\Delta x \, \Delta p' \geq h/2\pi$

where h is the Planck's constant. This inequality means that if you try to reduce the inaccuracy in position measurement, the inaccuracy of the measurement of momentum increases, and vice versa. Scientists believe that it is not the result of the limitations of the measuring instruments, but an innate law characteristic of the quantum world. To get an idea of this uncertainty, "suppose that the position of an electron is measured to the accuracy of one part in a nanometer (10^{-9} m), then the momentum would be so uncertain that one could not expect that, one second later, the electron would be closer than 100 kilometers away"[2].

This leads to subatomic particles behaving unpredictably preventing the physicist from tracing a particle's future behavior. Unfortunately, we cannot discuss this topic further.

11.4 Elementary Particles

By 1920, physicists had a fairly good picture of the nature of an atom. An atom consists of a nucleus containing positively charged protons and also (sometimes) neutrons which did not carry any charge. Around the nucleus were electrons in different "orbits" or "shells". The electrons moved around the nucleus at the speed of 600 miles per hour. These subatomic particles were called elementary particles.

As nuclear physics progressed, more and more "elementary particles" were discovered. At present their number is in excess of 200. Most of these particles are created in the laboratory where high speed (known) particles collide with one another.

Dirac predicted the existence of the anti-electron having the same mass as the electron, but the opposite (positive) and equal charge. This was later confirmed. This was followed by the discovery of many pairs of particles having opposite charges but the same mass.

When a particle and its antiparticle coalesce, both of them disappear and energy is created. When we try to divide a particle using high energy what we get is not smaller pieces, but two particles of the same type showing that the energy is converted into a twin. This may be shown as x + E = x + x

According to Capra, the subatomic particles are destructible and indestructible at the same time.[3]

Particle physics is now called high energy physics because high energy is required to bring about reactions. Most of these artificially created particles last for less than a millionth of a second. They either revert to stable particles, electrons, protons and neutrons or get converted into energy.

11.5 Virtual Particles

Because of extremely high speeds of subatomic particles, one has to use relativistic equations. While special relativity has solved some of the problems relating to particle physics, scientists have faced a few new problems.

One of the major problems is duality displayed by the field of force. The force between interacting particles is now perceived as an "exchange of particles". These particles are called virtual particles. The stronger the force, the higher is the probability of exchanging virtual particles. It is believed that even nucleons (protons and neutrons) may be emitting virtual particles. Thus field and virtual particles appear to be two sides of the same coin.

The dual behaviour of electrons can be found even when they are orbiting in an atom. They can be described as "standing waves".

The quantum world is ever changing. Its actors appear to change their roles constantly

Capra has captured the essence of this world succinctly :[4]

> The high energy scattering experiments of the past decades have shown the dynamic ever changing nature of the

particle world in the most striking way. Matter has appeared in these experiments as completely mutable. All particles can be transmuted into other particles ; they can be created from energy and vanish into energy. In this world classical concepts like elementary particles , material substance or isolated object have lost their meaning, the whole universe appears as a dynamic world of inseparable patterns.

What we witness in the quantum world is an incredible multiplicity where the identity or individuation of particle is constantly changing. This multiplicity is nothing but a manifestation of non-absolutism or relativism

A few subatomic reactions are given below:

(1) $n \rightarrow p + e + \nu$ (a)

This shows a "beta decay" in which a neutron decays into a proton (+), an electron (-) and an antineutrino ν (a) (the twin of the neutrino). The last is massless and difficult to detect.

(2) $0 \rightarrow p + \pi + p$ (a) $\rightarrow 0$

In the above, three particle are created from vacuum, proton, pion and antiproton. All these particles immediately vanish.

(3) $n \rightarrow n + \pi \rightarrow n$

A neutron emits (under certain conditions) a pion which is again absorbed by the parent neutron.

Let us try to express (1) in terms of *saptabhaṅgī* . Suppose the reaction begins at the time t and ends at t'; t'-t may be a fraction of a second. It is assumed that all necessary conditions are incorporated in the *syāt*.

1. From a certain point of view (*syāt*) the neutron exists (at t)
2. *Syāt* the neutron does not exist (at t')
3. *Syāt* the neutron exists (at t) and the neutron doe not exist (at t')
4. *Syāt* the neutron is indescribable.
5. *Syāt* the neutron both exists and is indescribable.
6. *Syāt* the neutron does not exist and is indescribable.
7. *Syāt* the neutron exists and does not exist and is also indescribable.

(4) arises because the physicist refers to (1) and (2) simultaneously which results in confusion and hence the neutron becomes "indescribable". (5) may be thought of when the physicist is primarily concerned with the neutron but is also aware of the reaction which makes the situation indescribable. Similarly when he is basically preoccupied with the result at t' but is also aware of indescribability, (6) may be said to arise. Finally, when he thinks in succession about the neutron and the three products, but is aware of indescribability, (7) appears to be the case.

Each of the reactions (2) and (3) can be looked upon as two different *saptabhaṅgīs* in succession. Or these two *saptabhaṅgīs* may be combined. For example, in case of (3), the combined *saptabhaṅgī* is :

1. *Syāt* the pion exists (at time t')
2. *Syāt* the pion does not exists (at time t, t")
3. *Syāt* the pion exists (at time t') and does not exits (at time t, t")
4. *Syāt* the pion is indescribable (with reference to simultaneity of its status at t' on the one hand and t, t" on the other), etc.

Reaction (2) is most striking in that the vacuum gives rise to particles which in turn leads to the vacuum. The vacuum is a creative vacuum which seems to be empowered to destroy its creation and resume the original status of apparent "nothing". Thus

1. *Syāt* the vacuum exists (at time t , t")
2. *Syāt* the vacuum does not exist (at time t')
3. *Syāt* the vacuum exists and does not exist.
4. *Syāt* the vacuum is indescribable, etc.

It should be worthwhile to observe that in each of these reactions "indescribable" does not merely indicate a formula-driven confusion created by simultaneous reference to existence and non-existence. It shows a truly inexpressible situation created by incredible behaviour of subatomic actors.

12. *Anekāntavāda* and Einstein's Relativity

12.1 Philosophy and Physics

It is time we made a comparative study of Jaina relativism or non-absolutism and Einstein's theory of relativity.

Jaina *syādvāda* or *anekāntavāda* is a very broad philosophy of non-absolutism. In fact as we will see shortly, it is embarrassingly wide or general, apparently bearing the stamp of an "absolute principle". Einstein's relativity covers a very narrow area of physics. It deals with space, time and gravitation which are shown to be non-absolute. It also has relativistic corollaries such as equivalence of mass and energy. The combined physics of relativity and quantum theory expands the realm of non-absolutism. Fields, particles, energy, etc. appear interconvertible. There is also transmutation of one type of particles into another.

12.2 Scope

Jaina relativism is objective and demands empirical evidence. It refuses to incorporate subjectivity (personal tastes and whims) into its *syādvāda*. From this angle it is similar to relativity physics. Unfortunately its growth seems to be arrested at some point. In his paper "Rudiments of *Anekāntavāda* in Early Pali Literature." Bhagchandra Jain mentions the following developmental stages of *anekāntavāda* :[1]

1. *Ekaṃsavāda-Anekāntavāda.*
2. *Sat-asat-ubhayavāda.*

3. *Avaktavya.*
4. *Saptabhaṅgī, and*
5. *Two-fold naya* and seven-fold *naya.*

However, its non-absolutism does not seem to have progressed beyond *saptabhaṅgī* which is treated as complete knowledge consisting of seven *nayas* which are usually treated as partial knowledge.

Anekānta cannot be treated as a hard science such as physics because it lacks a few features which characterize what we call narrow science. Quantification is a major feature of modern science. *Anekānta* has preferred to remain at the philosophical level.

An important feature of science is what Einstein calls "stratification of the scientific system".[2] As science progresses there is a march from special laws to general laws. For example, the orbits of planets can be studied with the help of Kepler's laws. The behaviour of falling bodies can be understood through Galileo's experiments. It was Newton who combined the works of Kepler and Galileo and presented a unified theory of gravitation.

In relativity physics itself there appears the following progressive history :

Galilean relativity → Special relativity → General relativity.

There is further integration of relativity with quantum theory and efforts are on to propound a Grand Unification Theory (GUT) in which all types of forces are integrated. Broadly there are four types of forces : (1) the gravitational which is extremely weak, (2) the electromagnetic forces which are stronger than the gravitational force, (3) the weak nuclear force which is responsible for radioactivity, and (4) the strong nuclear force which holds the components of the nucleus tightly. So far the gravitational force refuses to be integrated with other forces. It is a long way to arrive at a satisfactory GUT.

In case of Jaina relativism initially interaction with Buddhism seems to have started the process of integration which resulted in the five stages of development mentioned earlier. But further progress seems to be stymied. While many modern writers have tried to reconcile *saptabhaṅgī* with modern logic or modern science they seem to regard the "seven and only seven" formula inviolable. Even those scholars such as D. Bhargava ("A few Modern Interpretations of non absolutism") and R. Singh ("Relevance of *Anekānta* in Modern Times") who present unorthodox views seem to accept the magic figure of seven.[3]

The scope of *anekāntavāda* is so broad, it almost embarrasses an analyst—he is bound to arrive at the conclusion that everything is relative. Consider any meaningful statement "A is B" where A is the subject and B, an attribute. The following formula is valid :

1. *Syāt* A is B
2. *Syāt* A is not B
3. *Syāt* A is B and A is not B
4. *Syāt* A is inexpressible
5. *Syāt* A is B and inexpressible
6. *Syāt* A is not B and inexpressible
7. *Syāt* A is B, not B and is inexpressible

One does not have to prove the validity of this formula because the *syādvāda* principle asserts that a subject A has infinitely many properties and the seven-step formula is valid for countless attributes of A. A few grey areas may appear. First, the statement may be meaningless though grammatically correct, e.g. "Adversity stands on five legs." The septet should be used only when the statement "A is B" is meaningful. Second, in case of transcendental matters, a statement such as "God exists" may be considered irrelevant, having no place in Jaina epistemology. On the other hand it may be accepted in the form "God does not exist" as the First Step of the septet, reflecting Jaina atheism. But this statement is not empirically provable and a controversy is bound to arise. Similarly, a statement about rebirth is likely to create problems because Jainas believe in rebirth but such acceptance cannot be considered empirically validated.

The general conclusion is that *syādvāda* is applicable to almost all meaningful statements except those pertaining to the transcendental realm.

Compare this with relativity physics. It makes no claims about non-absolutism anything beyond the pale of a small region of physics.

It might be thought that if the First Step of *saptabhaṅgī* "A is B" is true, the next six steps may not follow in every context. This is not so. It is not at all a difficult task to form these steps. Remember a *syāt* statement is subject to determinants like place, time, etc. (chapter 4). One can think of scores of determinants and it is not difficult to choose some which for a certain value makes "A is B" true and for another value makes "A is not B" true. Once the first two steps are formed the remaining five follow automatically. In fact even if "A is B" is false we can treat "A is not B" as the first statement and its opposite "A is B" as the second. Given a particular "viewpoint" we can always create another "viewpoint" by manipulating determinants in such a way that "A is B" (first viewpoint) gets converted into "A is not B" (second viewpoint)

12.3 Seven and only Seven

In chapter 4 it was shown that *saptabhaṅgī* can be extended to twelve steps. In fact, with a few more permutations and combinations the number of statements can be extended indefinitely without changing the substance or fundamental philosophy. On the other hand, the first two statements

syāt A is B

and *syāt* A is not B

appear to be adequate to incorporate relativism. Since *avyaktavya* is interpreted as viewing "A is B and A is not B" simultaneously, the significance of statements 4 - 7 appears negligible though scholars have tried to explain their non-redundancy.

I will explain the loss of signinficance of *avaktavya* with reference to D. S. Kothari's paper "The complementary Principle and *Syādvāda*".[4] In Heisenberg's "thought experiment" there is a closed box in which an atom is placed. The box is divided into two equal parts by a partition which has a small hole through which the atom can pass. The hole can be plugged if necessary. According to classical epistemology, an atom cannot be at two places at the same time. However, quantum behaviour leads us to conclude that, the same atom can be in both the compartments at the same time. Kothari classifies this situation as *avaktavya*, he goes further and depicts the behaviour of the atom according to *saptabhaṅgī* as follows :

There are seven quantum states corresponding to the seven steps of *saptabhaṅgī*. Omitting quantum symbolism the steps appear as follows:

1. 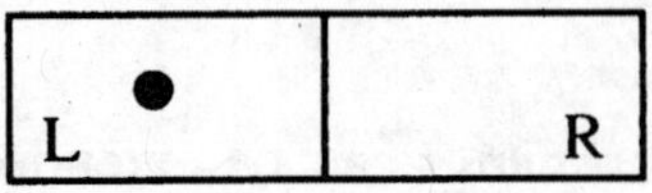

The atom exists in L

2. 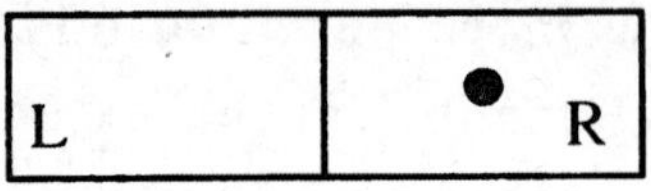

The atom does not exist in L (it exist in R)

3. 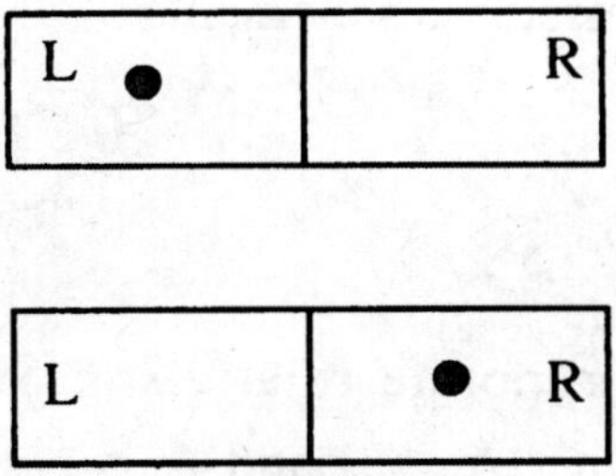

The atom exist in L (at one time) and does not exist in L (at another time)

4. 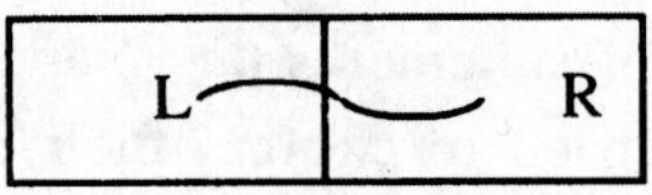

The atom exists and does not exist simultaneously in L (*avaktavya*)

5. (1) and (4) at different times — The atom exists in L and is inexpressible.

6. (2) and (4) at different times — The atom is not in L and it is inexpressible.

7. (1), (2) and (4) at different times — The atom is in L, it is not in L and it is inexpressible.

The fourth state above is truly inexpressible (*avakatavya*) because physicists are unable to determine the position of the atom due to particle-wave duality and uncertainty principle in quantum phenomena which we considered in chapter 11. Kothari, however, misses the central point of *saptabhaṅgī*, viz. the seven steps hold good for any subject and every attribute the subject possesses. *Avaktavya* is not reserved for a special case where the phenomenon is truly inexpressible. Jaina *avaktavya* is a simultaneous view of any attribute B and not-B. An assertion and denial *eo ipso* results in *avaktavya*. This is exactly why I called Jaina non-absolutism embarassingly broad. We will revert to this subject when we consider how *syādvāda* can be enriched in wake of modern science.

12.4 Social Dimension

While relativity physics has nothing to do with socio-cultural aspects of life, Jaina non-absolutism has social and ethical dimensions. The limbs of *anekāntavāda* appear to contain contradictory statements, but they not only constitute a philosophy but try to reconcile different views. The very concept of relativism is believed to reflect an attitude of tolerance and respect for others' views. Since Jainas are not dogmatic, their attitude towards other credos tends to be conciliatory rather than confrontationist.

Their philosophy of many sidedness asks you to be cautious and to consider an issue from different angles before you make an unequivocal statement clinging to one particular aspect.

Relativism is also believed to contain the germs of nonviolence or *ahimsā*. Weighing different sides of an issue engenders respect for others' views whence is born the desire to refrain from harming others physically or psychologically.

12.5 The Transcendent

Jainas are realists, objectivists and empiricists. They are also called atheist. Unfortunately the doctrine of *karma* and the idea of rebirth tend to introduce a transcendental dimension into their philosophy which otherwise is concerned with mundane phenomena intelligible to the layperson.

Relativity physics being a branch of hard science considers transcendental issues irrelevant though some scientists are believers (like Einstein) and some are atheists (like Hawking). Similarly, relativity physics considers ethics and socio-cultural issues beyond its ambit.

12.6 *Syādvāda* in Relativity

It is interesting to see how the statements of relativity physics would appear in the framework of *syādvāda*.

Suppose there are two inertial frames of reference S and S' moving at uniform velocity with respect to each other. A and A' are observers stationed in S and S' respectively, i.e. for A and A', S and S' appear stationary.

The *saptabhaṅgī* would appear as follows :

i. *Syāt* S' is moving (the viewpoint of A)
ii. *Syāt S'* is not moving (the viewpoint of A')
iii. *Syāt S'* is moving and not moving (i + ii)
iv. *Syāt S'* has indescribable movement (i and ii simultaneously)
v. *Syāt S'* is moving and is indescribable (i + iv)
vi. *Syāt S'* is not moving and is indescribable (ii + iv)
vii. *Syāt S'* is moving, not moving and is indescribable (i + ii + iv)

Here relative motion fits into *saptabhaṅgī* admirably. Compare this with an ordinary statement like "the pot exists". The *saptabhaṅgī* of this appears as a simple manipulation driven by a standard formula. But in the case of relative motion there is a real element of manifest surprise. For example, "S' is moving and not moving" is not only baffling, it is supported by objective description. Similarly, in "S' is inexpressible" the *avaktavya* appears truly indescribable inasmuch as the simultaneous superposition of moving and not moving is at once puzzling and real. Moreover, the physicist who is familiar with basic relativity has an insight into how the *avaktavya* actually arises.

The fifth statement can be looked upon as the one made by A who is preoccupied with the behaviour of S' but is aware of the strangeness of the superposition of "moving" and "not moving". The sixth statement is relevant to A' for whom S' is stationary, but who is also aware of the *avaktavya*. The last statement may be said to be relevant for a physicist who is neither on S nor on S', but is introspecting over the relative motion of S and S'. The above *saptabhaṅgī* is valid even in case of Galilean relativity which should be obvious even to a common person.

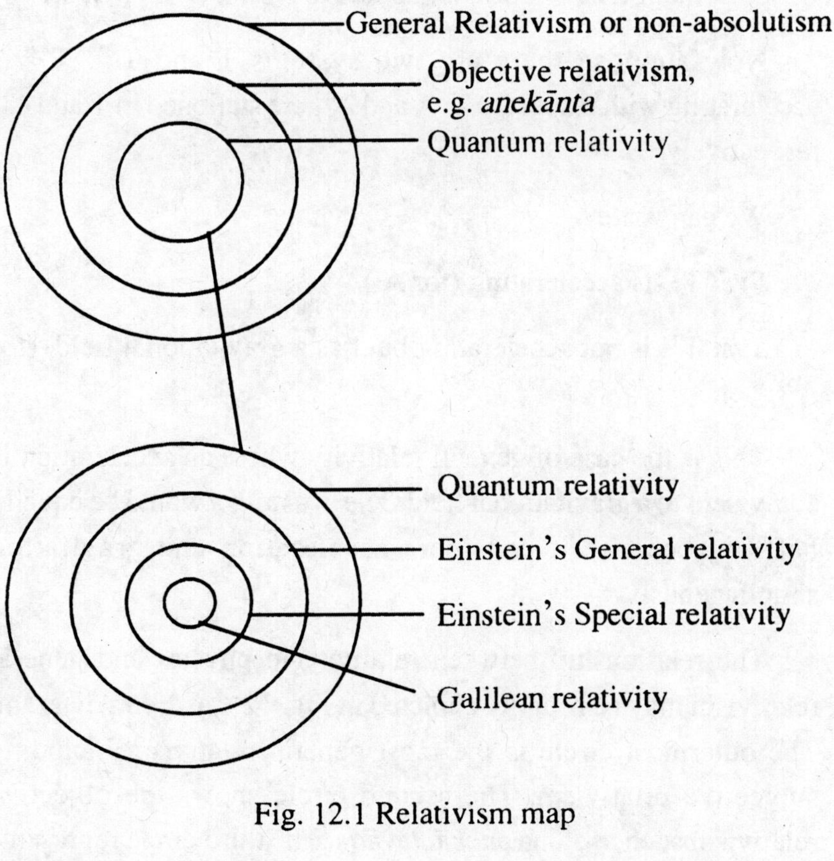

Fig. 12.1 Relativism map

With respect to Einstein's special relativity, the following septets would appear to be appropriate. Only brief statements are given below.

Time :

Syāt the clock in S' is slow. (with respect to A)

Syāt the clock in S' is not slow. (For A'.), etc.

Length :

Syāt the rod in S' appears to shrink. The shrinkage is maximum in the direction of its motion with respect to S (For A.)

Syāt the rod in S' does not appear to shrink (For A'.), etc.

Now suppose there are two systems T and T''. T'' is accelerating with respect to T. A and A'' are stationed in T and T'' respectively.

We can write :

Syāt T'' is accelerating (for A.)

Syāt T'' is not accelerating but has a gravitational field. (for A''.), etc.

This is the case of general relativity where an acceleration is equivalent to a gravitational field. The *avaktavya* would be equally baffling because it considers acceleration and gravitation simultaneously.

The relationship between relativity in physics and general relativism may be roughly depicted in Fig. 12.1 as Venn diagram. The outermost circle is the most general relativism including subjective relativism. The second circle shows the objective relativism such as Jaina *anekāntavāda*. The third circle represents non-absolutism of quantum relativity which should actually be shown by four circles; Galiean relativity is the innermost, special relativity appears next enclosed by general relativity and finally quantum relativity which is the outermost circle. Regions are shown as circles as a matter of convenience. Any outer circle has greater degree of relativism than an inner circle it encloses.[5]

When quantum physics is conjoined with relativity, the scope of non-absolutism expands considerably. At the micro level, quantum relativity reveals a large universe of objective relativity. Space and time are relative. The concept of a body at rest is illusory. Energy and matter are two sides of the same coin, and so are matter and waves. Different frames of reference whether uniformly moving or accelerated can be described in terms of Riemannian geometry where the curvature is zero in case of flat space-time and positive or negative in case of curved space-time. In the curved space-time acceleration and gravitation are non-absolute in the sense acceleration can be replaced by equivalent gravitational field and vice versa.

Most elementary particles especially those created in the laboratory lose the significance of identity since a set of particles may be converted into another set of other particles in a fraction of a second. Even what we call a vacuum loses its existential meaning since a pair of a particle and its anti-particle may suddenly emerge from the vacuum. We may say that non-absolutism is the general rule in the sub-atomic world.

However, to us the non-absolutism is not patent in the macro world we live in. While relativistic effects are perceived by physicists, and are significant for astronomical distances and high velocities, effects of quantum relativity are opaque to us and are inferred by a few specialists who work in the quantum world.

We may conclude this chapter by observing an essential difference between Jaina relativism and relativity physics. The former is based on creating different situations through linguistic manipulations such as varying predicates, changing determinates and so forth. Relativism is almost a priori. In the latter, relativity appears as a consequence of continual experimentation. This is obvious because relativity physics is a hard science.

13. Enriching *Syādvāda*

13.1 Introduction

There are two reasons which appear to have hampered the progress of the philosophy of *anekānta*. The first is generalization without differentiation. The second is inadvertent introduction of absolutes. I will shortly discuss these two aspects and try to explain how *syādvāda* can be enriched and aligned with modern science. Fortunately, Jainism believes in empiricism and objectivity. Relativism is the central theme of Jaina philosophy. My suggestions will not violate the basic tenets of either objectivity or non-absolutism.

13.2 Differentiation and Integration

It is interesting to observe how a child gains knowledge. The adherents of Objective Epistemology emphasize that the process of learning involves "differentiation and integration". To understand this process suppose the child is in contact with tables and chairs. He perceives similarities and differences in respect of their characteristics.

For example, a chair has a seat and a back and people occupy the chairs. He integrates the pronounced features of the chairs and their common use. This leads him to the concept "chair". Similarly he observes that tables are used for keeping small objects. He imbibes the common features of all tables and thus emerges the concept "table". These two concepts involve integration subsuming all tables in one concept and all chairs in another concept. It also involves differentiation of chairs on the one hand and tables on the other.

The process of differentiation takes the child further to distinguish subsets of chairs; reclining chairs, folding chairs, mini chairs for children, etc. Similarly, he is able to classify tables into "writing table", "dining table", and so on. The child also proceeds in another direction. In addition to chairs and tables he comes into contact with sofas, cots, cupboards, etc. which have a common feature; they can be moved. He soon gains the concept of a superset "furniture".

This process of differentiation and integration creates a hierarchy of concepts. Recall that in school biology we studied a similar hierarchy, species, genus, etc. The process, however, is not unidimensional. For example, all chairs may be used for sitting, but some of them are black, some are white, etc. Again, some may have arms while others are without arms. The child develops through abstraction a multidimensional network of concepts. While the child learns unconsciously, adults create sets, subsets and supersets consciously as the method of orderly classification in all branches of knowledge.

Anekānta, as I remarked earlier appears too general. It possibly began with one-stage "is", then went to two-stage philosophy, "is", "is not", thence to "is and is not" and later to simultaneous "is" and "is not" yielding *avaktavya* and further combinations reaching the seven-step *saptabhaṅgī*. At some stage it seems to have made a quantum jump and arrived at the seven steps which appears as the final stage.

Two observations need to be made. First, as the philosophy appeared to use integration, differentiation seems to have taken a back seat. The philosophers seem to have taken only one road "the linguistic route". *saptabhaṅgī* no doubt, involves relativism but one which is obtained by verbal manipulation that leads to the widest non-absolutism. It does not consider factually different cases which need to be distinguished.

Consider the following cases.

1. A group of persons encounters a strange animal. It has three legs and two faces (each resembling the face of a tiger) and four horns. No one from the group has ever seen such a creature before. "It is indescribable", they all agree.
2. A proton behaves like a wave and also like a particle.
3. An atom can be considered both as matter and energy.
4. Gravitation can be treated as a field of force or the cause of curvature of flat space-time.

What is the *avaktavya* in the case of a jar? It is merely an inexpressibility created by superposition of jar and not-jar, a formula-driven confusion that follows from superimposing contradictions.

But each of the four cases (1 -4) has *avaktavya* which is really mind-boggling and which has roots in new discoveries.

The first pertains to biology, and the rest to physics. The last represents geometrization of gravitation. We can think of at least a few main types of *avaktavyas* :

1. Routine *avaktavya* in which superposition of opposite attributes *eo ipso* makes the statement inexpressible.
2. *Avaktavya* involved in probabilistic (uncertain) occurrences such as "head or tail", in the toss of a coin.

3. Indeterminacy as appears in quantum theory and relativity such as matter-wave duality and matter-energy duality, or Heisenberg`s Uncertainty principle (chapter 11)
4. Transcendental statements such as relating to rebirth after death, God, etc.
5. The logical middle in Lukasiewiczien system (chapter 7.)
6. *Avaktavya* showing epistemic limitations. For example, a question such as "Did it rain yesterday at a place x in the deep forest?" when x is not accessible.

These categories are not mutually exclusive and categorization also depends on one`s personal opinion. For example, a transcendental proposition may be considered nothing but a subset of category (6). Again, logical middle may be considered merely a manifestation of epistemic shortcomings.

It is possible to consider *avaktavya* as a category involving all types of "inexpressible" in the fourth *naya* of *saptabhaṅgī*. But then it will cease to be mere simultaneous superposition of opposite attributes and its nature will vary from case to case. This will also modify steps (5) - (7) inasmuch as the connotation of *avaktavya* is enlarged.

It is possible that *avaktavya* of the traditional *saptabhaṅgī* has roots in inseparability of the opposites from psycho-linguistic point of view. However, the depth of *avaktavya* can be appreciated only when different cases of *avaktavya* are considered. What I am trying to suggest is that "inexpressible" has dimensions other than mere superposition of "is" and "is not" and its implication and true semantic status can be fully comprehended only when it is analyzed with reference to various situations.

13.3 Relativization

There is another direction in which *anekāntavāda* can move towards enrichment. It would be worthwhile to describe briefly Finkelstein`s approach to relativization.

It was mentioned earlier that one of the features of science is generalization. Finkelstein`s theory can be used to show how in relativity physics generalization has taken place.

Finkelstein`s approach is based on the analysis of Segal, Inonu and Wigner and shows how the concept of relativism can be enlarged in physics as well as in philosophy.

We will call this technique of relativization SIW ((after Segal, Inonu and Wigner). The method consists in identifying a "false absolute". An "absolute" is a property or an existent which is not observer-dependent; "relativity" is the term used in SIW to indicate that a theory implies that a phenomenon`s appearance is dependent on the observer. "Reification" means false identification of something as an absolute which in reality does not exist. An "idol" is an entity which is mistaken for an absolute through reification. Incidentally the word idol was first used by Francis Bacon in this sense.

A "simple" is an entity which does not include any other entity. A simple collection of simples is called "semi-simple". A "nonsimple" or a "compound" is an entity which is not semisimple. It may be called a complex. It consists of a simple which is subordinated to another dominant simple. Frankelstein offers a good example; a snake which has just swallowed a pig[1]. This is a one-way coupling; the relation between the dominant snake and the subordinate pig is not symmetric.

In Galilean physics space/time is a compound, space (position) being nonabsolute and time absolute. Here time is a potential idol. Now the task of relativization lies in searching for a symmetrical coupling which would put space and time on par. Constancy of the velocity of light, c, precisely plays this role. When this is incorporated into Einstein`s special relativity space-time becomes a symmetrical coupling.

However, with special relativity rises a new idol, viz. inertial systems moving with uniform velocity with respect to each other. The principle of equivalence which leads to general relativity demolishes this new idol creating a new two-way coupling between matter and space-time. Incidentally, there is a transformation of the Euclidean geometry (the idol) into non-Euclidean geometry.

13.4 Relativization in *Anekānta*

Anekānta already incorporates the principle of relativism. But is there an inadvertent tendency to treat any of its components "absolute"?. I think over the centuries philosophers have unconsciously tended to treat three features as absolute; *avaktavya*, "seven and only seven" statements and *saptabhaṅgī* itself.

Avaktavya is treated mechanically as superposition of a proposition p and its negative ~p (simultaneous view)

I have already mentioned how several types of *avaktavyas* can be distinguished.

The "seven steps" again appears to be an absolute. As we inspect these successive steps one by one, we find there is a gradual diminishing of reality. Though every step contributes to total knowledge, the contribution of successive steps decreases as we go down the steps. Each step takes us remoter from the kernel of total knowledge. I have shown earlier that a little manipulation can increase the number of steps. It looks that the *saptabhangī* can be expanded indefinitely, each additional wrung taking us remoter and remoter from the central truth, albeit contributing something to the total knowledge. The contribution of each incremental step continues to diminish.

Those of you who are familiar with infinite series can compare *anekānta* with the following series

$1 = 1/2 + 1/2^2 + 1/2^3 \ldots$

Each term on the right hand shows its contribution to the complete knowledge which is the left side , viz. 1. Each successive term is smaller than the previous terms, i.e. a term's contribution to total knowledge decreases as it moves further to the right. This is a mere metaphor and I do not wish to "prove" anything. I merely wish to point out that the doctrine of *anekānta* is based on the hypothesis that each entity has infinitely many attributes. The doctrine can be better appreciated if we are not rigid about the number of steps in the *anekānta* formula.

13.5 Provisional Nature of a Theory

A scientific theory is always treated as provisional. This provides an ample room for its modification when additional evidence is found necessitating a few changes in the theoretical model. There is no finality since scientific theories are based on inductive reasoning and hence are probabilistic. With every modification, the credibility of the theory increases.

To cite an example, recently physicists at CERN (European Centre for Nuclear Research) have found that neutrinos can travel with a velocity greater than the velocity of light. This needs further investigation before the scientific community accepts the results. In case, the observation is confirmed beyond doubt, it will ostensibly violate one of the corollaries of special relativity, viz. there cannot be a speed greater than c. In such a contingency c will appear as a false absolute and physicists will have to modify relativity theory in the same way that Galilean theory was superceded by special relativity.

The provisional status of a scientific theory reflects rational relativism or non-absolutism. Since Jaina scholars view *syādvāda* as objective non-absolutism, it should not be difficult for them to accept progressive modifications consistent with the spirit of *anekānta*.

14. The Enigma

A question now arises as to whether the doctrine of *syādvāda* or *anekānta* is itself absolute or relative. The analysis of *saptabhangī* leads to the conclusion that the seven-step formula is valid for any subject. In other words, the first step of the general *saptabhangī* can be written as :

Syāt x is a

where a is any attribute of x.

Concentrating on the general message of *syādvāda* we can write :

Syāt x is relative, where a is replaced by "relative".

In particular, if x assumes the value *syādvāda* or *anekānta* we get :

Syāt syādvāda (or *anekānta)* is relative.

This means *anekānta* at least under some conditions (*syāt*) becomes relative and ceases to have universal application. *Saptabhangī* is no more an authentic absolute formula. On the other hand, if we start with "anekānta is absolute" where "a" is replaced by "absolute", as the First Step, it militates against its very essence, viz. "every thing is relative".

This is a blind alley and recalls the well-known liar's paradox in logic. We may try to avoid the paradox by suggesting "every thing is relative except *anekānta*". This may technically resolve the paradox. But the new proposition makes *anekānta* a dogma which is against the very spirit of *anekāntavāda,* making Jaina philosophers vulnerable to the charges of dishonesty.

Matilal calls *anekānta* a "meta-metaphysical position". But he cannot avoid an antinomy. "Above all the Jainas were non-dogmatic, although they were dogmatic about non-dogmatism"[1].

Such linguistic conundrums involving complex logic can only lead to more confusion. If we listen to the central message of *syādvāda* or *anekānta* we will have to concede that this doctrine does not accept stasis. Its very spirit makes the principle relative and hence liberal and receptive to modifications as the world changes. This is also consistent with modern scientific thought, viz. a theory is always provisional and never final. This is amply demonstrated by relativity physics which has undergone many modifications.

Synopsis

Jaina Non-absolutism

Non-absolutism or relativism is one of the pillars of Jainism. This philosophy is known as *anekāntavāda* (*anekānta* for "not one end") and *syadvāda* (literally, "the doctrine of somehow").

Einstein`s theory of relativity is one of the two revolutionary theories of physics born in 20th century, the other being quantum theory. There are many similarities between relativity physics and Jaina relativism as well as other eastern and western relativistic philosophies.

This book discusses the similarities and differences between relativity physics and philosophical relativism with special reference to Jainism. It endeavors to dispel some misconceptions harboured by many people who tend to equate relativistic philosophies with relativity physics.

Jainas believe in objectivity and empiricism. They regard the mind as an instrument of discovering reality. They do not accept a priori arguments unless empirically proved. The Aristotelian laws of the mind, viz. the law of identity, the law of excluded middle and the law of contradiction are not accepted a priori but as empirical facts based on experience.

Jainas regard reality as multifaceted. This has led to the doctrine of *anekāntavāda* and *syadvāda* which may be called the doctrines of non-absolutism or relativism. They have devised a seven-step formula called *saptabhaṅgī* which gives complete knowledge of an object under consideration. If, for example, the object is a pen, the seven steps appear as :

Syāt the pen exists; *syāt* the pen does not exist; *syāt* the pen exists and does not exist; *syāt* the pen is indescribable (*avaktavya*); *syāt* the pen both exists and is indescribable; *syāt* the pen does not exist and is indescribable; *syāt* the pen exists, does not exist and is indescribable.

Every statement is subject to the prefix *syāt* which means "from a certain point of view". This philosophy is thus the philosophy of different standpoints. Each of these statements is partially true while the seven steps together convey complete knowledge of reality. In the above statements, "and" is used to indicate successive applications of sub-statements. For examples, the third statement "the pen exists and does not exist". The fourth statement, however, is an exception, the word "indescribable" or *avaktavya* should be interpreted as simultaneous reference to "exists" and "does not exist". This simultaneous superposition of contradictory predicates leads to the pen appearing as inexpressible.

The prefix *syāt* to every statement is absolutely necessary. For example, the pen exists (in Mumbai) and the pen does not exist (in Kolkata) happen to be true because of the proviso *syāt*.

Most Jaina scholars believe that seven steps are necessary as well as sufficient to express *anekāntavāda*. However, we can show that using permutations and combinations of "successive" and "simultaneous" views *saptabhaṅgī* can be expanded without much difficulty.

Syādvāda and *Nyadvāda*

The word *syādvāda* is often treated as synonymous with *anekāntavāda*. However, historically *syādvāda* appears to have started with two statements, e.g. "the jar exists" and "the jar does not exist". Other statements were gradually added later to reach the stage of *saptabhaṅgī*. In this development interaction between Jainas and Buddhists played an important role.

A doctrine closely related to *anekānta* and *syādvāda* is *nayavāda*. Usually *naya* is interpreted as a single step in *saptabhaṅgī*. Each *naya* is partially true while *saptabhaṅgī* asserts the whole truth. However, some commentators such as Malliṣeṇa regard *nayavāda* as consisting of seven steps or seven viewpoints which are structurally different from the *saptabhaṅgī* mentioned above (called *saptabhaṅgī-pramāṇa*) Malliṣeṇa calls this septet *saptabhaṅgī-naya*. The seven viewpoints projected in *saptabhaṅgī -naya* are *naigama, saṃgraha, vyavahāra, ṛjusūtra, śabda, samabhirūḍdha and evambhūta*.

Anekānta as Logical System

Many scholars have tried to express *anekānta* and *syādvāda* in pure logical frames. For example, Pandey attempts to use Lụkasiewicz's three value logic in which *avaktavya* appears as the third value. Gokhale has contented that Kleen`s system is more useful. Barlingay has suggested use of modal logic. Segarmal Jain and B. Matilal have tried conditional propositions for various *nayas*. Gokhale has suggested a model using the existential quantifier. I have myself tried a model based on relational calculus. However, all these models appear inadequate to express *syādvāda* using symbolic logic. The reason is that Jaina non-absolutism contains not only pure logic but also epistemology and ontology. Use of symbolic logic does not bestow any special advantage such as brevity nor does it provide motivation or tools for further research.

Galileo and Einstein

In pre-Einstein era most physicists believed in absolute space and absolute time. It was assumed that a rigid body followed Euclidean geometry. If P and Q are points in space with space coordinates x, y, z and x', y', z' respectively, then the distance PQ is given by

$$PQ^2 = (x - x')^2 + (y - y')^2 + (z - z')^2$$

This is constant for all observers. Similarly, if two events occur at times t and t`, the interval t` - t is the same for all observers.

Galileo observed that a ship at rest and one moving with uniform velocity cannot be easily distinguished if you are in the ship. If you watch flying creatures, fish in water in an aquarium or water dropping from an inverted bottle when the ship is at rest, these phenomena continue to appear the same when the ship is moving with constant velocity. Galileo`s observation leads to a great insight, viz. of the bodies moving with uniform velocities with respect to one another, no particular body can be called the body at rest. This is Galilean relativity.

Before Einstein, Newton was accepted as the greatest physicist. He considered light as a beam of fast moving particles. However, some phenomena like interference could not be explained by his corpuscular theory. It was therefore proposed that light consisted of waves. An allied theory of fields was successfully propounded by Faraday to explain magnetic and electric phenomena. It was Maxwell who proposed that light and other electromagnetic waves consist of magnetic and electric fields propagating at a constant velocity c. In 1887 Michelson-Morely experiment confirmed that light travels with constant velocity c irrespective of the observer's location or velocity.

Special Theory

Einstien's special theory of relativity is based on the fact that the velocity of light is constant. When we consider observers moving with uniform velocities with respect to one another, we cannot treat any particular observer as at rest. This is a modification of Galilean relativity in that c is treated as constant.

Many equations in dynamics are altered and many mind-boggling results follow from Einstein`s theory. For example, a moving clock appears to go slow, a moving rod appears to shrink in the direction of motion. Mass and energy appear to be interconvertable according to the famous equation $E = mc^2$.

In pre-relativity physics the interval (distance) is constant for all observers. In special relativity the interval includes a time component. What is constant is

$$S^2 = (x - x')^2 + (y - y')^2 + (z - z')^2 - c^2(t - t')^2$$

which is called the space-time interval. This equation holds good when gravitation is ignored. This is called a Minkowskian world of four dimensions having three space coordinates and one time coordinate. The above equation shows the fours dimensional "flat world."

General Theory

Einstein soon realized that special relativity unnecessarily restricted physics to the select frames, viz. inertial systems. Why should we not include systems other than those moving with uniform velocities? He considered accelerated systems and reasoned that an accelerated system could not be distinguished from an inertial system with gravitational field. This is the principle of equivalence.

Einstien argued that a body has two different masses. The first is the gravitational mass which is affected by an applied gravitational force; the second is the inertial mass which resists this force. Because of the unique nature of gravitation these two masses are equal. This is reflected in Galileos' discovery that the gravitational acceleration is independent of the mass.

General relativity thus integrates space, time and gravitation all of which appear relative. Consideration of gravitation implies that the space having gravitational field is "curved" and not "flat". The invariant space-time interval replaced by ten equations is shortly written as

$$ds^2 = \Sigma g_{\mu\nu}\, dx_{\mu}\, dx_{\nu}$$

where $g_{\mu\nu}$ is a "tensor". These equations involve squares and products of "dx"

Quantum Relativity

A theory closely related to relativity is quantum theory whose effects are substantial in the micro world of sub-atomic particles. In this theory one finds that light and elementary particles such as electrons have dual personality; they behave like matter as well as waves. Quantum experiments show mind-boggling results. The principle of uncertainty suggests that you cannot simultaneously measure a particle`s momentum and position accurately. If you try to be more accurate in respect of one parameter, the other becomes more inaccurate. The quantum world is incredibly bizarre. In a vacuum there suddenly appear a particle and its antiparticle which may soon disappear. In fact it is difficult to assign a permanent identity to many particles and follow their life history.

Relativity when combined with quantum theory displays a micro world which is the epitome of non-absolutism. In quantum relativity almost everything is non-absolute.

Mass and energy are non-absolute. Matter and wave are relative. Gravitation and acceleration are relative. Space and time are relative. The concept of "rest" becomes meaningless.

The various instances of non-absolutism can be expressed in the form of *saptabhaṅgis*

Jaina Relativism and Relativity Physics

It is interesting to compare Jaina relativism with relativity physics. Both swear by objectivity, rationality and empiricism. However, unlike relativity physics, Jaina philosophy contains transcendental topics such as rebirth and the doctrine of karma. This is exactly why Jaina *anekānta* cannot be called hard science.

Anekānta is a broad philosophy. In fact it is embarrassingly broad because given any subject and its predicate *saptabhaṅgī* can be formed using different determinants. *Saptabhaṅgī* is based on a standard formula involving mere linguistic manipulation. It is so broad that any aspect of relativity physics can easily fit into the *saptabhaṅgī* formula. Relativity physics on the other hand is confined to a narrow area. This area can be expanded by conjoining quantum theory at the subatomic level giving us quantum relativity.

Most Jaina scholars accept *saptabhaṅgī* formula as sacrosanct. In fact it can be proved that *saptabhaṅgī* can be expanded beyond seven steps. Even modern scholars who try to incorporate modern knowledge and thought cling to "seven and only seven steps". This is one of the reasons why Jaina relativism appears stagnant. Relativity physics on the other hand is open to revision in the light of new discoveries.

Syādvāda has a social dimension. Based on different points of view, it asks you not to be fanatically attached to your personal view. This philosohy leads you to tolerance and *ahiṃsā* or non-violence. Respect for others' views implies that you should refrain from harming those who do not agree with your views. Relativity physics, of course, is not concerned with morality and ethics.

Jaina *syādvāda* can be enriched in several ways. First, the notion of *avaktavya* needs to be analyzed. At present it is used as a standard simultaneous superposition of the opposites such as "is" and "is not". This is an omnibus "indescribable" created at the psychological level. Scholars must recognize the situations which are truly startling which appear especially in science. Some examples of such *avaktavyas* are : a proton behaves like a particle as well as a wave, matter can be treated as energy and vice versa, an accelerated frame of reference can be regarded as a stationary frame with gravitation and so forth.

Another way of enriching *syādvāda* is by identifying "false absolutes". A false absolute is one which appears as absolute, but in fact is relative. Relativity physics discovered many such false absolutes; absolute time and space, stationary objects, acceleration and so on. All these absolutes were relativized. In *anekānta saptabhaṅgī* is a false absolute : it can be shown that the number of steps in this formula can be increased. In other words *saptabhaṅgī* can be relativized. It must be recognized that the very spirit of *anekānta* militates against accepting "seven and only seven steps" as a dogma.

A liberal approach to *syādvāda* also solves the puzzle : is *syādvāda* itself an absolute doctrine? This question leads to a paradox similar to the famous liar's paradox. But if we sincerely accept the central message of *anekāntavāda* and *syādvāda* we have no option but to conclude that this philosophy is itself relative. This attitude leaves ample space for Jaina philosophy to grow and align itself with modern science.

Chapter Notes

1. Introduction

1. Relativism is present even in apparently perfect discipline such as mathematics. There can be a relative zero or a variable zero. Again, a number such as 5 can be treated as a natural number, a positive integer, a rational number or a real number. For mathematicians these different avatars of 5 have different existential statuses. See Burde (2009), chapter 8.

2. Jainism

1. Basham, p. 291.
2. The doctrine of *karma* ("action" or "work") in Indian tradition implies that a person's actions lead to reward or punishment depending on the nature of actions. The accumulated *karma* is carried over to the next life. In Jainism *karma* has a physical appearance.

3. The Mind and Knowledge

1. Mookerjee, p. 11.

4. Non-absolutism or *Anekāntavāda*

1. Quoted by V. M. Kulkarni in "Relativity And Absolutism", Shah (ed.), p. 61.
2. Mookerjee, pp. 119-20.
3. Ibid., p. 128.

4. B. K. Matilal in "*Anekānta* : Both Yes and No", Shah (ed.), p. 14.
5. See Kulkarni, "Relativity and Absolutism", Shah (ed.), p. 61n.
6. Mookerjee, chapter V.
7. Ibid., p.112.
8. See, for example, Burde (2009), pp. 23-25, 77-78.
9. Theoretically the elements +, -, 0 can be arranged in 3 x 3 x 3 = 27 ways assuming each type can be repeated. Between each such arrangement x and y can be inserted in 2 x 2 = 4 ways. Hence we get 27 x 4 = 108. Similarly, +, -, 0 taken two at a time give 9 x 2 = 18 arrangements. There are also three one-element arrangements. Add all these arrangements and subtract two arrangements + y - , - y + which give 0 and we get 108 + 18 + 3 - 2 = 127 steps. But if we assume commutative and associative laws, viz. ab = ba and a(bc) = (ab)c, the number of steps can be reduced depending on our assumptions. Again, some duos (among trios) may yield 0 = + y -, - y + which will reduce the number further. It all depends on which combinations are considered distinct and which are treated as identical.
10. Shah (ed.), pp. 67-74.
11. Ibid., pp. 73-74.

5. *Syādvāda* and *Nayavāda*

1. Atsushi Uno in "A Study of *Syādvāda*", Shah (ed.), p.35.
2. Quoted by Uno, ibid., p. 35.
3. Uno's comments, ibid., pp. 36-37.
4. Quoted by Uno, ibid., p. 41.

5. Ibid., p. 51, the account is based on Uno's quotations from various sources.
6. Ibid., p. 52, the account is based on Uno's quotations from various sources.
7. Ibid., p. 52.
8. Ibid., p. 52.

6. Jainism and Buddhism

1. Bhagchandra Jain in "Rudiments of *anekāntavāda* in Pali literature", Shah (ed.), p.119.
2. Ibid., p. 120.
3. Ibid., p. 120.
4. Ibid., p. 121.
5. Ibid., pp. 123-24.
6. Ibid., p. 124.
7. Ibid., p. 125.
8. Quoted in K. Venkata Ramanan, p. 158.
9. Ibid., p. 161.
10. Ibid., p. 163.
11. Quoted in Ichimura, pp. 359-60.
12. Ibid., p. 359.
13. Quoted in Ichimura, p. 360n.
14. Quoted in ibid., p. 372n.
15. This is consistent with Dignāga`s theory of *apoha*.
16. Burde (2012) discusses this functional aspect in chapter 10.

17. Mookerjee, p. 192
18. Ibid., p. 194.
19. Mookerjee, p. 210.

7. *Anekānta* As a Logical System

1. Pradeep P. Gokhale in "The Logical Structure of *Syādvāda*", Shah (ed.), p. 75.
2. Ibid., p. 76.
3. Ibid., p. 79, quoted from Rescher`s *Many-Valued Logic*.
4. Ibid., p. 79.
5. Quoted by Gokhale, ibid. p.80n.
6. Ibid., pp. 84-85.
7. Ibid., p. 85.
8. Ibid., p. 86.

8. Pre-relativity Physics

1. S. Drake quoted in Penrose, p. 163.

9. The Theory of Special Relativity

1. Penrose, p. 192.
2. Bergmann, p. 40. A length which is perpendicular to the direction of motion is not affected.
3. Quoted in Penrose, p. 193.
4. A detailed discussion on this topic will be found in Penrose, pp. 193-99.
5. Hawking, p. 29.

10. The General Theory of Relativity

1. Einstein (1956), p. 54. Newton thought "time is absolute, space is absolute". According to special relativity, "space-time continuum is absolute".
2. A similar case appears in another instance of the inverse square law in magnetism.

11. Non-absolutism in the Quantum World

1. Penrose, p. 235.
2. Ibid., p. 248.
3. Capra (1993), p. 89.
4. Ibid., pp. 91-92.

12. *Anekāntavāda* and Einstein's Relativity

1. Shah (ed.), p. 126.
2. Einstein (1979), p. 293, in his paper "Physics and Reality".
3. Shah (ed.), chapters 9 and 11.
4. Ibid., pp. 87-94.
5. Medieval Indian philosophers and mathematicians had considerable insight into the concepts of space, time, finitude and infinity. Unfortunately they could not develop calculus which is an indispensable tool in higher physics. They seem to have almost reached the concept of limits, the foundation of calculus, but evidently missed the boat.

13. Enriching *Syādvāda*

1. Burde (2012) has discussed the matter of relativization at length in chapter 31, "Universal Relativity"

14. The Enigma

1. "*Anekānta* : Both Yes and No", Shah (ed.), p. 16.

BIBLIOGRAPHY

Ahlfors, L. V. (1966). *Complex Analysis*. Kogakusha, Tokyo.

Bag, A.K. (2003). *The Concept of Śūnya*. IGNCFTA, INSA, Aryan Book International, New Delhi.

Band, William. (1964). *Introduction to Mathematical Physics*. Affiliated East-West, New Delhi.

Basham, A. L. (2001). *The Wonder That Was India*. Rupa & Co., New Delhi.

Bergmann, Peter Gabriel (1969). *Introduction to the Theory of Relativity*, Prentice-Hall, New Delhi.

Berne, Eric (1968). *Games People Play*. Penguin, Middlesex.

Burde, Jayant (2012). *Buddhist Logic and Quantum Dilemma*. Motilal Banarsidass, New Delhi.

_____(2007). *Philosophy of Numbers*. Munshiram Manoharlal, New Delhi.

_____(2004). *Rituals, Mantras and Science: An Integral Perspective*. Motilal Banarsidass, Delhi.

_____ (2009). *Śūnya and Nothingness*. Motilal Banarsidass, New Delhi.

Capra, Fritjof (2003). *The Hidden Connections*. Flamingo, India.

_____ (1976, 1993). *The Tao of Physics*. Flamingo, London.

_____ (1983). *The Turning Point*. Flamingo, London.

Chopra, Deepak (1993). *Ageless Body, Timeless Mind*. Harmony Books, N. Y.

_____ (1990). *Quantum Healing*. Bantom N.Y.

Deshpande, Dhanajay (2001). *Vedanteel Vidnyan*. Popular Prakashan, Mumbai.

Durant, Will (1953). *The Story of Philosophy*. Pocket Books, New York.

Eddington, A.E. (1924). *The Mathematical Theory of Relativity*. Cambridge University Press, London.

Einstein, Albert (1979). *Ideas and Opinions*. Rupa & Co., Calcutta.

_____ (1956). *The Meaning of Relativity*, Oxford IBH, Calcutta.

Hawking, Stephen W. (1989). *A Brief History of Time*. Bantam, N. Y.

_____ and Stephen, Roger Penrose (1997). *The Nature of Space and Time*, OUP, New Delhi.

Ichimura, Shohei (2001). *Buddhist Critical Spirituality : Prajñā and Śūnyatā*. Motilal Banarasidass, New Delhi.

Kirtishinghe, B. P. (ed. 1984). *Buddhism and Science*. Motilal Banarsidass, New Delhi.

Krishnamurti, J., David Bohm (1985). *The Ending of Time*. Krishnamurti Foundation, Chennai.

Laanen, M. V. (2004). *Encounters with Infinity:A Metamathematical Dissertation*. New Age Books, New Delhi.

Matthews, P. T. (1968). *Introduction to Quantum Mechanics*. Tata McGraw-Hill, New Delhi.

Mookerjee, Satkari (1978). *The Jaina Philosophy of Non-absolutism : A Critical Study of Anekāntavāda*. Motilal Banarasidas, New Delhi.

Page, Leigh, N. I. Adams (1955). *Principles of Electricity*. S. Chand & Co. Delhi.

Penrose, Roger (1991). *The Emperor`s New Mind*. Penguin, N. Y.

Peterfreund, Sheldon P., Theodre C. Denise (1968). *Contemporary Philosophy and Its Origins*. East-West, New Delhi.

Rajam, J.B. (1960). *Atomic Physics*. S. Chand & Co., Delhi.

Rand, Ayn (1990). *Introduction to Objective Epistemology*. Meridian (Penguin), N. Y.

_____ (1984). *Philosophy. Who Needs It*. Signet (Penguin), N. Y.

Russell, Bertrand (1999). *History of Western Philosophy*. Routledge, N. Y.

_____ (1948, 1992). *Human Knowledge*. Routledge, London.

_____ (1994). *Mysticism and Logic*. Routledge, London.

_____ (1995). *The Analysis of Mind*. Routledge, London.

_____ (1992). *The Principles of Mathematics*. Routledge, London.

_____ (1988). *Logic and Knowledge*. Routledge, London. (N.Y.).

Salmon, Weseley C. (-) *Logic*. Prentice-Hall, N.J.

Shah, N. J. (ed. 2000). *Jaina Theory of Multiple Facets of Reality and Truth (Anekāntavāda)*. Motilal Banarsidass, Delhi.

Sharma, R.N. (2004). *Text Book of Symbolic Logic*. Surjeet, Delhi.

Simmons, G. F. (1963). *Introduction to Topology and Modern Analysis*. McGraw Hill, N. Y. (Kogakusha Tokyo).

Smith, Huston (1991). *The World`s Religions*. HarperCollins, New Delhi.

Stcherbatsky, Th. (1963). *Buddhist Logic Vol. I-II*. Motilal Banarsidass, New Delhi

Staal, Frits (1996). *Ritual and Mantras : Rules Without Meaning*. Motilal Banarsidass, New Delhi.

Sterling, S. G. (1958). *Electricity and Magnetism*. ELBS and Longman, London.

Tigunait, Pandit Rajmani (1983). *Seven Systems Of Indian Philosophy*. The Himalayan International Institute of Yoga science and philosophy of the U. S. A., Honesdale.

_____ (1999). *Tantra Unveiled*. The Himalayan International Institute of Yoga science and philosophy of the U. S. A., Honesdale.

_____ (1996). *The power of Mantra & The Mystery of Initiation*. The Himalayan International Institute of Yoga science and Philosophy of the U. S. A., Honesdale.

Venkata Ramanan, K. (2002). *Nāgārjuna's Philosophy*. Motilal Banarsidass, New Delhi.

Verma, K. D. (2008). *Vedic Physics : Towards Unification of Quantum Mechanics and General Relativity*. Motilal Banarsidass, New Delhi.

Wallace, B. A. (ed. 2004). *Buddhism and Science*. Motilal Banarsidass, New Delhi.

Wayman, Alex (1998). *A Millenium of Buddhist Logic*. Motial Banarsidass, New Delhi.

Woodroffe, John (1997). *The Serpent Power*. Ganesha & Co., Madras.

Index